MW00616983

ENCOUNTERS
—— WITH ——
WISDOM

❖ BOOK THREE ❖

ENCOUNTERS
— WITH —
WISDOM

❖ BOOK THREE ❖

Thomas Hora, M.D.

The PAGL Foundation
Old Lyme, CT

Published by the PAGL Foundation
P.O. Box 4001, Old Lyme, CT 06371

Copyright © 2011 by the PAGL Foundation

All rights reserved. No part of this publication may be reproduced or transmitted in any form or by any means, electronic or mechanical, including photocopying, recording, or any information storage or retrieval system, without prior permission in writing from the publisher.

Manufactured in the United States of America.

ISBN 978-1-93105-206-1

Contents

Introduction

This book is the third in a series of short volumes that continue to present Dr. Thomas Hora's Metapsychiatric teachings through dialogues with his students. Dr. Hora, the founder of Existential Metapsychiatry, was a pioneering psychiatrist whose work provided hermeneutic clarification of psychological issues in the larger context of existential and spiritual wisdom and understanding. He passed away in 1995, and his work lives on.

The selection of dialogues from the 1980s and 1990s remains fresh and helpful. We are fortunate that Dr. Hora tape-recorded most of his weekly group sessions with his students and made them available to those who attended. The Board of the PAGL Foundation[1] has collected many of the tapes and transcribed some of them. They have then been carefully edited to guarantee participant anonymity, improve readability, coherence and relevance, and to assign a title to each based on the principal theme of each meeting.

---

[1] PAGL is an acronym for Peace, Assurance, Gratitude and Love, qualities of consciousness that are the fruit of spiritual progress. The PAGL Foundation was established to make the work of Dr. Hora available. Previously published books consisting of group dialogues are *Dialogues in Metapsychiatry* and *One Mind*. Basic books by Dr. Hora on Existential Metapsychiatry are *Beyond the Dream* and *Existential Metapsychiatry*. These and other books, tapes and CDs are available from the PAGL Foundation and its bookstore (see *www.pagl.org*).

At each session Dr. Hora would enter the room and sit at the front of a circle of students. He would quietly look around the room, smiling at each participant. Someone would begin by asking a question or presenting a problem. Sometimes no one spoke up and Dr. Hora began by seeking to discern what was on peoples' minds.

The dialogues proceeded with Dr. Hora encouraging the students to shed light on whatever issue had been raised, and shifted when some participant found the need to bring up another topic. Everything flowed, and there was never pressure to continue discussing any single issue. At the end of each session the students left with a new understanding.

Encounters with Wisdom is your invitation to join that dialogue.

I

Political Correctness

Student: In an office environment, there is a term quite frequently used — "politically correct"— and as you progress you have to play politics and whatever else there is. In looking at that term, it seems to me that everyone tries to manipulate everyone else to accomplish whatever their goal is. In dealing with some of the senior executives, I am not always sure when it is appropriate to respond and when it is not. When something comes up, it sometimes seems provoking, and sometimes it is intimidating and I can't discern when it is appropriate to say something and when it is not appropriate to say something. I just can't tell. When I am dealing with people that I work with every day it is easy; the issue is the issue. But I can't always tell what the issue is at their level of management. Is it just an issue of making a power statement? I am not sure how to respond to that. I ruminate about it because I would like to understand it and I really don't. I don't know how I fit in. I am not used to dealing with that level of management.

Dr. Hora: Perhaps it would be helpful to start by asking, "What is the meaning of this new fad phrase 'politically correct' that has become fashionable?" What is the meaning of that phrase and the use of it? What do people mean when they use this phrase?

Student: You are supposed to think a certain way on issues. You are expected to agree with something and if you don't, you are stupid or conservative or old-fashioned. It means being in tune with the fashion.

Dr. Hora: Being in tune with the fashion. Political fashions. Okay, all right. There is a book called "Nineteen Eighty-Four." It was written by Orwell, and I remember years ago you had to be sexually conforming to the culture. It was an anti-sex book. In order to be a well-adjusted, healthy person, you had to be against sex, yes? Sex was a no-no, a politically incorrect way to participate in society at that time. Now it is reversed. Now if you want to be a real upstanding citizen, you have to be either homosexual, or a transvestite, or a harasser of women, or a transsexual. You have to have at least one operation on your genitals, or you have to have some legal action against your extra-marital activities, all the way up to the President. He is also in trouble, because his sex life is politically correct. You see, if he didn't have any scandal around his sex life, he would not be politically correct. He would not be in tune with the spirit of the times, right?

How did this phrase, "politically correct" come about? People have a desire to have clout. You know what clout is? It is a hammer with which you can hit somebody over the head, and you have to know something with which you can intimidate somebody in order to accuse him of not being politically correct.

During the time of the Nazis, if you had a drop of Jewish blood in you, you were not politically correct. You were out of it. During the inquisition in Spain, if you did not publicly proclaim yourself a Christian, you were not politically correct, and it had social consequences. Now people have a desire to be able to intimidate each other through some kind of a slogan or phrase. During Communism in Russia, and today in Iran, if you are on the street and if you smile, you are politically not correct. You can be arrested and jailed. So what is this thing that is tormenting the human race at various times and various periods with all kinds of accusations? If you live in Greenwich Village and you are not homosexual, you are not politically correct. You don't fit in. So when somebody is accused of being politically not correct, he is being accused of non-conformism, yes?

Who determines what is politically correct and what is not correct? The Antichrist. The Antichrist wants people to be confused and live in fear and live by standards and values that have nothing to do with God or reality. In various circles you have to be agnostic or anti-God or anti this or with this or with that. So whenever somebody speaks to you about being politically correct, what can you do? There is one statement that cuts across all these shenanigans, and that is the famous words of a great philosopher who said, "Bullshit." When anybody talks to you about being politically correct, you say "quatz." If you speak Japanese, you say "quatz." If you are full-blooded American, you say "Bullshit." It is always the pressure to conform that results in all kinds of stupidities of the Antichrist, which wants to get you so confused that you lose sight of spiritual values. Because if somebody says you are not politically correct, you are not living by the accepted norms and values of the American culture at this time. In Iran, you have different standards and values. There, you have to conform to the Ayatollah. Here, we have to conform to the bullshit artist, of which we have millions in the culture. Different parts of the city have different politically correct modes of thinking, acting, and behaving. It is such a sad sight, how the frightened people are tyrannizing each other through certain slogans. It is not politically correct to be anti-sex. You have to be for sex and you have to be for kinky sex. If you are just for straight sex, you are out of it. (laughter)

You see it is crazy—absolutely crazy, and the remedy is to have a firm anchoring in spiritual values. If you know what is existentially valid, nobody can frighten you with these slogans, whether or not it is politically correct. It is ridiculous.

Student: It sounded to me as if she was saying, if she has new supervisors who are asking her to do things that are for their personal pursuits of power rather than for what is needed on the job, she seems to have difficulty in knowing how to respond to these seemingly invalid requests by supervisors.

Dr. Hora: Of course. What would you advise her?

Student: The need is always to discern the issue, and if it is not clear what they are asking, ask, "What is the issue here?"

Dr. Hora: That is right, and no matter what anybody believes as to the political correctness, you have a right and you can never go wrong if you stand with integrity for what is right in the sight of God. Suppose your boss or your superior wants you to commit a crime or falsify some records. To be politically correct, you would have to go along with that, yes? So don't argue. You say, "This is the truth."

Student: That seems okay because I know from a point of integrity that would not even be an issue. But if my boss says to me that it is politically correct to cut staff and I don't agree with him, because we cannot meet the agenda and tasks at hand if he cuts the staff, ...

Dr. Hora: Isn't that ridiculous? Politically correct to cut the staff whether the bank will function or not. This is irrelevant.

Student: They are looking to save money. He got mad at me because I told him the truth.

Dr. Hora: What did you say?

Student: I said it didn't seem possible to work with that number and accomplish the same goals.

Dr. Hora: So you have no problem with this idiotic phrase.

Student: So, I got scared because I am not in conformity. He said, "You know every other manager that I said this to would say, 'Keep me posted,' but not you."

Dr. Hora: The hell with what is politically correct. What is right?

Student: I felt that was right. Then he wanted me to fire someone who has been there a long time because maybe he thought he could get somebody better. I said that was not appropriate. Then how do I not get scared? He is still my boss. I still have to report to him.

Dr. Hora: It is not politically correct to be intimidated. If you understand that God is your boss and God is your life and God is your good, then "God's grace is your sufficiency" (2 Cor. 12:9). Nobody can touch you; you cannot lose. It is no use to argue with these people about it. You just stand fast. This is it. This is right. That is all.

I remember one of you had a job where the employer, the boss, was forever trying to prove that you were wrong and he was right, and as long as you were trying to convince him that you were right and he was wrong there was a constant struggle, constant chaos, constant aggravation. Now, if you are a student of Metapsychiatry, you know it makes absolutely no difference who is right and who is wrong. The only thing that matters is, "What is the truth?" You see, the truth is always politically right. But don't tell it to anybody; they won't believe you. Unenlightened people see life in terms of interaction; we look at life in terms of the Truth of Being. We are not interested in who is right and who is wrong, but in "what is that really is?" Then there are no more arguments, and the stupidities of the culture and the various groups are not relevant to our lives.

I hear stories about arguments on college campuses. These are youngsters who have no experience with life, and they know nothing; all they know is relationships. They cannot see beyond relationships; so they are forever arguing about who is right and who is wrong. That is where it started, this craze, and now it has entered into corporate life. But it was essentially a juvenile effort at proving oneself superior to the next guy. We can forgive college students, because they don't know much and their mental horizon is rather constricted to the level of personalities. They see life in terms of interaction of personalities. They cannot even think in terms of truth or error, valid or not valid, and if you can't see beyond personalities, how far do you see?

Student: If you are not politically correct, then you are ostracized socially.

Dr. Hora: And that is bad? What does it mean when somebody is concerned about being ostracized, circumcised, socially? (laughter) It means that he functions on the level of personality, that personhood is the main issue in that life. How far can you get that way?

Student: Getting along with people...

Dr. Hora: Nobody can get along with people. You can hide your animosities and judgments; but is that getting along with people? You are becoming a bullshit artist and pulling the wool over other people's eyes, or writing fancy Christmas cards and brown-nosing. Do you know what that means? That is how people live who do not have a solid foundation in reality.

"Because thou hast made the Lord, which is my refuge,... thy habitation, there shall no evil befall thee, neither shall any plague come nigh thy dwelling." (Psalm 91:9) Nowadays, if you become socially ostracized like the President is now...He is being socially ostracized; he is politically correct; his popularity will rise. Michael Jackson, he is being ostracized, and the money is just pouring in. Everywhere you see this idiotic thing—being politically correct. Being a child molester is very popular. Sexually harassing women is terrific. Senator Packwood is a famous man. He is politically correct.

Student: Isn't it politically correct to treat women with a certain respect, and Senator Packwood is abusing them?

Dr. Hora: If you treat women with respect, the culture says you are just nobody, just a scared person who is avoiding notoriety.

Student: My idea of being politically correct: if you meet a woman who is an avowed advocate of women's rights and is campaigning, and you agree with her, then you are being politically correct.

Dr. Hora: No. You will fight with her.

Student: Then you are not being politically correct, because you don't agree with this issue.

Dr. Hora: The issue is not to agree or not agree. "Politically correct" means that you are involved in whatever is the fashionable thing at that time. To be inside families for a man, this is good. To be a feminist for a woman, this is also good. This is politically correct. Conflict is politically correct. Everybody has to be unhappy with everybody else and that is politically correct. Harmonious coexistence is ridiculous. Nobody is interested in that.

I was told about a Broadway show where everything occurred in jail, with cruelties and sexual abuse, and it became a famous show. It is a great success. It was called *Kiss of the Spider Woman*. Did you see this show? The more depraved and the more crazy it is, the more politically correct.

Student: You said earlier that it is the Antichrist that is adding confusion. What does that mean?

Dr. Hora: The Antichrist says there is no God. You are God. Only you matter: how you feel, and how you are socially adjusted. Psychologists established a norm. To be mentally healthy, you have to be well adjusted to society. Now if the society is sick, and it is apparently quite sick, you cannot afford to be healthy, because then you will be socially ostracized. You will be labeled politically not correct.

Student: If we want to fit in and be politically correct, then is the main problem that we are sacrificing spiritual integrity?

Dr. Hora: Absolutely. The Antichrist is working in that direction, to separate us from conscious at-one-ment with God.

Student: So if we are in a social situation or a business situation where there is a lot of temptation to be negative in order to fit in, then we don't want to antagonize and make a stand against it, and we can't agree because then we are sacrificing integrity.

Dr. Hora: Yes, you can't agree and you can't disagree. This is not politically correct but it is spiritually valid.

Student: So it doesn't matter what the particular cause may be that is politically correct at the time. It is the whole idea of conformity and not being tyrannized. Part of what seems to be politically correct is respecting various ethnic groups, not showing prejudice.

Dr. Hora: If you are spiritually correct, there are no ethnic differences. There are only perfect manifestations of God. Nothing else will ever bring peace and harmony into the world until people recognize this. Racial tolerance doesn't solve the problem. If I am tolerating you in this group, is that politically correct? It may be, but underneath I think you shouldn't be here because you have gray hair or who knows what. Now we live in an insane world, which was always insane from the beginning of time. The world was insane and the source of tribulations for all people who didn't understand what really is.

Now, what does it mean "political?" What does the word "political" mean in the phrase "politically correct?" What does the word "politics" mean?

Student: Does it have something to do with people?

Dr. Hora: Exactly. When the majority of people believe in a certain thing and you accept it and you take it for reality, you are politically correct but existentially insane. People don't realize it when they throw around slogans like that and don't analyze the words that they are using.

In a democracy we have politics as a standard form of behavior; but what does democracy focus on? Majority votes. You can be as crazy as can be, but if the majority of people agree with you, you are politically correct. In a democracy nobody is interested in the truth. We are interested in the power of the majority of votes.

Not long ago at a psychiatric convention, I think it was in San Francisco, they brought out the question for psychiatrists to vote on whether homosexuality is normal or a sickness. All the psychiatrists got so intimidated by the pressure from the community that they voted that homosexuality is not a disease; it is normal. How in the world can you decide the diagnosis on the basis of voting? You cannot vote on that. That is no solution. That is politically correct for us to tolerate various forms of sexual aberration and behavior. It is politically correct and even humanistically desirable.

We have to have compassion for people who take in poisons through the nose. Snorting cocaine is taking poison into the body through the nose. Many people do that, and they are very insistent on the idea that this is good. Now you take a thousand psychiatrists and say you have to vote that this is normal; otherwise, you are not politically correct. So you vote that this is normal. This is good. That is the democratic way.

Of course, democracy is not to be sneered at. It has its practical value in terms of peace and more justice than in authoritarian governments. And corruption is more under control through the democratic process, in which there are various ways of checking and double-checking, and there is freedom of the press and freedom of expression. We have the freedom to call each other names, and everything is more out in the open, whereas in dictatorships everything is tyrannical and suppressed. Unfortunately, neither in democracy nor in dictatorships is there an appreciation of the Truth of Being. Somebody said that democracy is a very bad form of government but is better than anything else that has yet been devised, which is true. So, thank God we have the freedom to be politically correct. It's just a ridiculous thing. "Let not your heart be troubled, neither let it be afraid" (John 14:27). Take a stand on the truth, the Truth of Being, and no evil shall befall thee, neither shall any social ostracism hurt thee.

Student: We were invited to see a show, and we were put in a situation where our consciousness was being defiled just by opening our eyes. If we were going to take a stand for the truth, we really should have picked ourselves up and left and not sat there. Are there other factors involved? The people who invited us to this probably were not aware of the harm that they were doing. Is kindness not hurting your host's feelings...

Dr. Hora: Yes.

Student: ...or compassion or just understanding that they don't understand, or is there some other consideration? Does it make your response different? Somehow it just doesn't seem right to just leave. I am not comfortable with that...

Dr. Hora: Yes.

Student: ...although I know that you hurt yourself by staying in that setting. I just can't seem to get comfortable with the alternative.

Dr. Hora: Yes.

Student: We said in the past that if you watch with disinterest, you won't be affected.

Student: It is difficult to watch *Kiss of the Spider Woman* with disinterest. It is not that you would be interested, but to see these visual effects is so degrading and disgusting. Even when the curtain rose initially, the first impression—the whole stage was filled with prison bars, and from the moment it began you knew you had just entered hell as a spectator, and pretty soon you are not a spectator anymore.

Dr. Hora: You get sucked in.

Student: Even if you are not interested. It is just terrible.

Dr. Hora: Somebody said to me earlier, "I didn't want to leave because they would have thought I was rejecting them." I said, "You would not have been rejecting them. You would

have been running away from them, and that is legitimate."
You have a right to run away.

Student: It doesn't seem loving.

Dr. Hora: Loving? You don't have to love evil. Since when do you love evil?

Student: Isn't the other individual going to be personally hurt?

Dr. Hora: It is good for them to be hurt, because they are perpetuating an aggression against a friend whom they invited to watch this abomination against God.

Student: I had a similar situation a long time ago. In that situation, I stayed. I was ashamed to get up and leave. I got a terrible headache. I had no idea about what the meaning of the headache was. But now I know that when I am invited to see a play, I need to find out what it is about, and, if I discern the content to be invalid, I can just refuse the invitation in advance, and not go. To go is torture. You are embarrassed to get up and walk out.

Dr. Hora: It is very interesting. Some students of Metapsychiatry pick up certain ideas—for instance, we had here a member of this group who suddenly discovered the power of Love. Whenever somebody said something with which she didn't agree, she didn't say, "You're politically incorrect." She said, "It is unloving." She was always throwing out, "This is not loving." That was her way of using politically incorrect. That was what she learned in Metapsychiatry. That is all. She came for about 15 years, but then she had a weapon to use against her friends and the family. She simply just threw out this, "This is not loving." That settled the whole thing. Nobody could say anything, because you are supposed to be loving, right? That is another example of bullshit.

Then there was a man, who after years of studying Metapsychiatry, picked up the word of "judgment." "You are judgmental." Every time somebody said something which he didn't like, he wouldn't say, "This is politically incorrect." He would say, "You are judgmental." This is what he learned. This is what he got for his money for years of studying Metapsychiatry.

Everybody is looking for a weapon. Nowadays you can buy guns—bingo. But if you don't want to shoot, you pick up a slogan and then beat people over the head with that slogan: "You are judgmental." "This is not loving."

Student: So if our consciousness is in jeopardy, it doesn't really matter how it affects anyone else. We have to remove ourselves to preserve...

Dr. Hora: Right. We are responsible for the quality of *our* consciousness. We are not responsible for what other people are interested in, and we have no right to tell people, "You should be loving." Who are we to tell people they should be loving? Haven't they ever heard of the Second Principle? Nobody says in Metapsychiatry that you should be loving. We only talk about what love is. That is all. We talk about what politics is. Politics is the quest for votes. Power through votes , and everybody wants power, even these people who say, "You are not loving."

Student: It is pretty amazing how people, or individuals, survive. We live in such a crazy state.

Dr. Hora: They don't survive very well. You read the papers and watch television. You see all the people who are victims of crimes, of family strife, of envy, jealousy, rivalry, malice, gossip—all the evils of the world that people are open to if they are ignorant. The most dangerous thing in life is to be ignorant. You don't know what is going on, and you don't know what is hitting you, and being a student of Metapsychiatry is no guarantee that you won't fall and pervert this study to conform to the culture in which we live. People want to have a weapon. If you don't want to use a gun you can use Metapsychiatry. (laughs)

Student: In the teachers' lounge at school, there is a cross section of all the things that go on in New York. There are homosexuals and blacks, and everybody is very sensitive about their own private, ethnic, or religious issues. It is like a minefield. Just try to say something in this room. It occurs to me that if you are clever enough to be politically correct, you can manage to get along with everybody in the room just by saying something innocuous. It is all baloney.

Let me ask you: Harmonious coexistence—how would it be possible in a situation in this room where people are barely tolerating each other? I have given up going to that room—it is just too tense—so, I stay in my office.

Dr. Hora: Nobody is missing you? (laughter)

Student: Is he protecting himself by not going in?

Dr. Hora: Who is *he*? (laughter) We are not dealing with personalities.

Student: If you are in a situation like that, and if you remove yourself from the situation, are you not being protective of yourself?

Dr. Hora: I don't get your question.

Student: I think I am just avoiding the situation. I don't know how to handle it, so I just stay away from it because I can't transcend it. Every time I go in there and I speak honestly, I get in trouble. (laughter)

Dr. Hora: And if you don't say anything, you are hiding something. Did you vote today? (laughter) You are not allowed not to vote. There is pressure to vote. Sometimes, no matter who you vote for, it is not valid anyway. "In this world ye shall have tribulations, but be of good cheer there is a way to overcome the world." (paraphrase of John 16:33) We cannot speak, and we cannot not speak.

Student: What can we do? We can know something, I suppose.

Dr. Hora: Yes, right. That is neither loving nor not loving.

Student: Is that spiritually correct? (laughter)

Student: What is the meaning of a sense of obligation? I am more and more aware that it is a false sense. Participating in gatherings that are held at holiday times—things like that, so often they just seem vacuous. They don't seem meaningful. But to not go seems, well, not politically correct. (laughter) Can you help me with that?

Dr. Hora: Yes, the question was: What is the sense of obligation we seem to feel in certain situations? Who can answer that question?

Student: Isn't the issue wanting to belong to something? To conform? It seems when an obligation is an issue, we want something, to be a part of something. So it is a false sense of obligation.

Dr. Hora: The sense of obligation is a disguised way of trying to be politically correct. Jesus never said you have an obligation to be spiritually minded. Can you imagine Jesus saying that? He would have meant that you should be spiritually minded. We don't say that, and he wouldn't have said that. He just said: "This is what is, and that is all there is."

Student: A sense of obligation is just a lot of "shoulds." It seems somebody else is telling us what we should do, but very often we are telling ourselves we should.

Dr. Hora: Right. You are either loving or not loving. You have an obligation to be loving, even if you hate. That is what some religions are implying.

Student: You could take the Second Principle and say: Take no thought for what you should *do* or should not *do.*

Dr. Hora: Sure. Always the "should" is the culprit complicating life. You should be this way. You should do this; you should not do that. You should go to church, and you shouldn't go to this place or that place. That is the essence of this phrase "politically correct." It is a "should" that people throw on each other.

Student: I think the part that causes uneasiness is the judgmentalism.

Dr. Hora: Yes, like the other student who learned to accuse people of being judgmental. He was always judging everyone about judgmentalism. (laughter)

When we said that prayer is the sincere contemplation of the Truth of Being, did we say that you are obligated to be sincere? One of our students came back with the question, "But how do you be sincere?" You see he immediately translated that statement about prayer into "should." You are required, you are obligated, you should be sincere, and I don't know how to do it because I am not really sincere. There is this tendency in the human consciousness to twist everything around in terms of what should be and what should not be. What is required? Nobody said that you should be sincere. We just gave a definition of prayer. We didn't say you should pray or you must pray, that it is your obligation. If you are a good Christian, you have to do this or do that. If you are a good Jew you have to eat chicken soup. Nobody said these things, right?

2

Overcoming Personhood

Student: I completely forgot about God taking credit. Saturday morning I was walking along, feeling happy and thinking that I looked wonderful, and I was very proud of myself. I didn't realize all this. I was just feeling wonderful, and then I twisted my leg. I asked myself, "What could be the meaning of this?" I wasn't angry and I didn't have any interaction thoughts. I was talking to a friend and she said, "Pride cometh before a fall." (laughter) It was not like she said it over the telephone. It was like it came from a loudspeaker. It was another lesson for me, a painful one that is still not completely healed. But Dr. Hora, when I recognize and I regret, it seems that though I am regretting, I am really regretting for the wrong reasons. I regret because I hurt myself and I was stupid. That's not enough. I have to understand that I am regretting invalid thoughts and I have to go to the second intelligent question and really understand it. It's difficult because I keep feeling the pain and I am more concerned with whether the pain is leaving than with understanding. What is my question? My question is, "Do I have to go on being ignorant and go on having these lessons and forgetting who I am and why I am here? Does it go on forever?"

Dr. Hora: The question is whether you are concerned about not having pain. Listening to you reveals that you seem to be primarily concerned with not having pain in your leg. If that is your concern, then you are on the wrong track.

Student: Yes, I know that the bottom line, no matter what the problem is, is being here for God and understanding that I am not a person but a manifestation of God.

Dr. Hora: No, the bottom line is that it is not good to be proud.

Student: Oh. (laughter)

Dr. Hora: You need to see that this is intellectualism. You overlooked the pride issue, and you regret the pain in your leg. You regret this, and then you think "What should I do? I should do this. I should think those thoughts." This is an operational approach to the question, "How should I be?" or "How could I be without this pain?" You go to a doctor and he will bandage the foot and give you an injection and give you crutches and then you will be without the pain. He will give you x-rays and put you under a scanner and make tests, like blood maybe. It's AIDS. (laughter)

Student: It was so obvious, as soon as I heard the word "pride."

Dr. Hora: What is needed is to be healed of pride. Isn't that so?

Student: It's so simple. (laughter)

Dr. Hora: Whenever people have a problem, whether a pain or some other problem, the primary thought is "How can I get rid of this problem?" The simplest thing is to get drunk or take a pill, or go to the hospital, and that is the simpler solution. It is very intelligent and rational, seeking how to get rid of the pain. So let's not forget that we are not primarily concerned with relief. There were two girls on TV. One said, "I have a headache," and the other immediately said, "Take two." She did not even say two of what; but everyone is supposed to know that it means two Anacin tablets. This is the way the world operates. Get relief, immediate relief. And then we're ready for the next episode. We can go from one problem to another and most people usually do. But people will say, "I have been studying so many years and I am still having problems. There is no end to it." Now how can there be an end to problems if you are interested in the problems? We are not interested in fast relief. Nor do we cherish pain. But unless we understand the meaning in order to get healed of that particular erroneous thought, we need to recognize that the healing has to take place in consciousness, not in "my foot." If it is not healed in consciousness, it is not healed. And even if there is relief, the potential for further problems remains. And so it can be that no matter how long you study Metapsychiatry, you just go from one problem to another. You can find relief one way or the other, but the question remains, "How can one be healed of pride?" Pride is more common than the common cold. It is almost ubiquitous. But nobody likes to deal with that. It is somewhat embarrassing to admit that we have a problem with the sense of personal pride.

Student: From the human perspective, pride is looked upon as being good. It leads to self confidence. So it is easy to get confused.

Dr. Hora: Yes, who in his right mind would want to be healed of pride?

Student: Right, because it is thought that you do not see yourself in a positive light if you are not proud of what you have accomplished in life. So much seems to be riding on pride.

Dr. Hora: So what's a mother to do?

Student: Study Metapsychiatry.

Dr. Hora: It's not enough to say that. You have to study Metapsychiatry the right way. If you do not study Metapsychiatry the right way, you won't get to the point where you are free of these problems. Pride, ambition, vanity—these are the three musketeers of Metapsychiatry. (laughter)

Student: What does it mean to study Metapsychiatry the right way?

Dr. Hora: Studying Metapsychiatry the right way means facing up to the meaning of our problems, be they ever so embarrassing. It requires radical sincerity. That is the first step. Unless you are willing to be embarrassed, you will never be free of this.

Student: As you study Metapsychiatry, it is so embarrassing to have a problem because it shows that you don't understand. Instead of my taking credit, I didn't see that the only good is God and God is the only good. It was me taking all the credit and isn't that pride?

Dr. Hora: Yes, we define pride as a desire to take credit. But how can we be healed of this desire? Every human person has a natural desire to take credit for whatever he accomplishes in life. It is a very strong motivating factor. People will work day and night and produce tremendous works of art, or anything, just to get credit. So Metapsychiatry says, "Listen, you have to give it up." Then we think that if I didn't have the satisfaction of getting the credit, I wouldn't do anything. I would become a bum. Nobody would have any motivation to work or to produce anything good. Don't you see people with medals and with all kinds of awards? What are all these awards, like Teacher of the Year, etc.? Everybody feels good when he or she gets recognition and awards. It's normal; it's human; it feels good. And everybody is willing to knock himself or herself out to get that. So isn't it ridiculous for anyone to be asked to be healed of pride? Pride, ambition, and vanity are wonderful human aspirations. (laughter) What are you laughing at? I'll tell you a secret. As long as you see yourself as a human person, you will never be healed of the three musketeers. (more laughter)

Student: It seems that no matter what your problem is, that's the answer.

Dr. Hora: What's the answer?

Student: Seeing yourself as a person.

Dr. Hora: What's wrong with that?

Student: As long as we see ourselves as persons, we are subject to the dualism of the three musketeers, which is equally painful. I mean pride seems okay if we have something to be proud of.

Dr. Hora: Is that so?

Student: Well, in a human sense, pride seems good.

Dr. Hora: Whatever feels good is good?

Student: Yes, but the other side of the coin is shame, and that's not good.

Dr. Hora: It is not good because it doesn't feel good. (laughter) You see how intelligent we are. How did this student get herself embroiled in this ridiculous argument? Whenever we reason from the standpoint of personal sense, we are in trouble. Personal sense says that whatever feels good is good. Whatever doesn't feel good, like a leg pain, is not good. Isn't that very rational, logical and self-evident common sense? So what's wrong with it? It doesn't get you anywhere. The more you subscribe to this belief, that whatever feels good is good and that whatever doesn't feel good is not good, the more you are a simpleton. What's a simpleton? It's somebody who doesn't really understand life, one who judges by appearances and doesn't go beyond what seems to be. A normal human person is a simpleton.

Okay, so then the problem is that we believe that we are human persons who are happy, unhappy, smart, stupid, or something else. What other possibilities are there? If we are not human persons, we could be animal persons. What's an animal person?

Student: Would it be just reacting according to our instincts?

Dr. Hora: Yes. An animal person is fascinated by his physical sensations, and he is a pleasure seeker. He is even more convinced that whatever feels good is good, and he goes by that. There are all kinds of complications that animal persons experience. You can be an animal person, or you can be a human person. A human person wants to be proud, ambitious, vain, jealous, envious, malicious, and smart. He has personal mind power to influence other people the way he wants and is constantly involved in interaction processes. That's a human person. In order to be healed of these things, we have to rise to a higher level of consciousness where we discover that we are not really those things. We are spiritual beings, transparencies for God. Our idea of the good is not physical and it is not mental. It is spiritual. In order to realize that, we have a principle. What kind of principle do we have?

Student: Reality cannot be experienced or imagined; it can only be. . . .

Dr. Hora: I knew you would miss it.

Student: The first principle?

Dr. Hora: The first principle says the good of God is spiritual blessedness, which is the supreme good of life. But a human person has no idea what it is. Now suppose somebody is an intellectual and intellectually ambitious. Is that a human person or a spiritual being?

Student: It is a claim of personal mind.

Dr. Hora: Right. If we are intellectually ambitious we confuse enlightenment with intellectual verbiage. We can talk about things that enlightened people know, but we don't know. We have just read about it. Let's be clear that intellectualism is still on a human personal level. It is not superior to anything else. It is just another aspect of pride, ambition and vanity.

There is intellectual vanity; there is accomplishment vanity, as well as pride and ambition. It is very important to know where we stand in order to be healed of all these problems of being a normal human person. These problems are endless.

Student: Sometimes it seems like it can never be cleaned up all at one time.

Dr. Hora: It gets cleaned up in one swoop. How does it get cleaned up in one simple swoop?

Student: Letting go of a sense of personhood.

Dr. Hora: Yes. Wholeheartedly seeking to realize spiritual existence, which is non-corporeal, which is transparent, which is divinely created, maintained and inspired, moment to moment. We are spiritual beings; we live and move and have our being in the divine mind. And all communications are from God to man. We lose the sense of personhood and cease to be interested anymore in all those things in which human persons are interested. So there is no more pride, ambition, vanity, or interaction thinking. What is there?

Student: Omniaction.

Dr. Hora: Omniaction. What is that? What is omniaction?

Student: Communication from God?

Dr. Hora: Communication from God to man. That is a mode of being-in-the-world which is out of this world. Jesus called it "having overcome the world." He said that we must overcome the world, which means that we must rise above the sense of personhood. We must lose interest in all those things in which human persons are interested.

Student: We have this idea that when we come here, we might not have pride, in the sense of showing off. I don't know if this is just semantics, but it is easy to think of yourself as a person, and it seems you can get stuck as a person this way. You think of yourself all the time in terms of personal problems.

Dr. Hora: Yes. Very good. Excellent point. There are many sincere students who try to spiritualize their personhood. And what have you got then?

Student: Nothing, just another problem.

Dr. Hora: You have a human person who talks spiritual language, but has not realized it.

Student: But isn't it necessary to start there?

Dr. Hora: Well, if you want to start there it is okay, but it is time to move on...

Student: After 40 years. (laughter)

Dr. Hora: The crucial word is interest. What are we really interested in when we are studying Metapsychiatry? Are we interested in learning a new language made up of spiritual words and remaining persons? Or are we interested in ascending to the conscious awareness of ourselves and of others as spiritual beings governed by the divine mind?

Student: It does seem that when we face up to the meaning of a problem, and it takes a long time, we are stuck at that level, then, of being persons...

Dr. Hora: Who said it takes a long time? It's instantaneous. All it takes is to be radically sincere and to understand where you are going.

Student: Radical sincerity comes from God also.

Dr. Hora: No, it comes from pain. If you are in pain, first you want to find relief. And if you find relief today, today you will run into another pain and that will go on until you run into a pain that becomes intractable. When it becomes intractable, you become interested in radical sincerity. And when you are sincere about radical sincerity, you will be willing to face up to the meaning of your pain. From then on you become interested in attaining a consciousness which is beyond the personal level. It is called a transcendent consciousness, or the Christ consciousness, where the three musketeers are not present anymore, and you see yourself as having risen to a level where you understand that you are not a human person.

Student: Is it possible that some of us do not have the capacity to be radically sincere?

Dr. Hora: These people have to come to Dr. Hora to get a statement that says they are constitutionally defective and unable to achieve... (laughter)

Student: Dr. Hora put it this way, "All you have to do is bring the check and leave."

Student: How is it that embarrassment can be so important along this path? It seems like such a human emotion. Recognition, I suppose, comes from God, because if we have the opportunity to see how different things seem from the way they really are, that makes some sense. But embarrassment is such a human emotion. How can embarrassment be helpful?

Dr. Hora: It's painful and pain and suffering are absolutely necessary for progress in life. Nobody who is happy makes any progress. You know who are the happiest people? The mentally retarded. Nobody envies them. Nobody feels threatened by them. They just live within their limitations. But if we do not have the blessings of mental retardation, (laughter) we are obligated to struggle for progress, like the caterpillar who is obligated by its very nature to get out of the pupa stage and become a butterfly. We have to struggle to achieve the Christ consciousness, which is above the sense of personhood, where there is no more pride, ambition and vanity. There is nothing but humility. There is just "Is." Have you been in the land of "Is?" God said, "I am that I am," which means I am that which is, which means nothing else that seems to be really is. (Exodus 3:14) Only I am. So whether we like it or not, we struggle to achieve that level of consciousness, and if we fail, we have to come back and start all over again.

Student: Oh, God forbid. (laughter) A higher level or a lower level?

Student: Is transcendence awareness? Are they synonymous? I was reading in one of the booklets that awareness is incorporeal.

Dr. Hora: Well, awareness is a faculty of consciousness to be conscious of its content. Transcendence is a form of awareness of having risen above the conventional modes of thinking where normal human persons function in the world. That is what it is.

Student: Could we say spiritual awareness?

Dr. Hora: Yes, it is a transcendent awareness, a faculty that we all have. We just have to wake up to it.

Student: Did you say, "I am is"? Is that what you said?

Dr. Hora: I am what is.

Student: And the I am is spiritual qualities?

Dr. Hora: No, "I am the being that really is." God said that to Moses. "I am that I am" means "I am the being that really is."

Student: Isn't God a spiritual quality? How then do we get to being? I do not understand.

Dr. Hora: God is much more than spiritual qualities. But God is recognized by spiritual qualities. God is infinite mind, infinite power, infinite creativity, infinite love, infinite in everything real, immutable, and infinite. That is God.

Student: Is that what you meant when you said, "even beyond humility?"

Dr. Hora: Humility is still a human experience.

Student: So the saying, "I can of my own self do nothing" (John 5:30) is still referring to the person, but is acknowledging the presence of God?

Dr. Hora: Right. Enlightened man does not have to be humble. Jesus sometimes gave the impression that he was arrogant. He said, "I am the way, the life and the truth. No man cometh unto the Father but by me." (John 14:6) Many times he referred to himself. If we were very unsophisticated, we would be under the impression that he was bragging. As a matter of fact, some of the audience he was talking to objected to this way of talking. "The Pharisees therefore said unto him, 'Thou bearest record of thyself; thy record is not true." (John 8:13) And he said what?

Student: "My record is true: for I know whence I came, and whither I go." (John 8:14)

Dr. Hora: Right, he knew the truth of his being; therefore, he didn't have to be humble and neither did he have to be arrogant. He just tells it like it is. He just said, "What Is is." That's the way it is. Walter Cronkite also said that.

Student: Is he describing his awareness of himself?

Dr. Hora: Yes, "I am the light of the world; he that followeth me shall not walk in darkness." (John 8:12) That is a great self-confirmatory sentence. "I am the bread of life; (John 6:35) he that understandeth me shall never hunger. I am the water of life; he that drinketh of this water shall never thirst." (John 4:13-14) There are many such patently self-confirmatory statements, but he wasn't confirming his human personhood. He was confirming his spiritual understanding of all mankind, because we all have to reach there eventually. I don't know how long it will take, but we all have to get there. This is an existential fact, and nobody is exempt from this process. It's not too bad. It's okay to be on the spiritual path. It is very interesting.

Student: Is that the only valid way to be on the spiritual path? Is the right way with the motivation of seeking understanding?

Dr. Hora: Seeking to understand is the highest level of consciousness, which is called enlightenment, or the Christ consciousness, or the Buddha Nature or Howdy Doody.

Student: I think the thing I was driving at before, (laughter) when I made a fool of myself, is the idea, which you've told me at least a thousand times, perhaps ten thousand times, that radical sincerity is required, and that without radical sincerity you will not get anywhere. Yet I find that when I am by myself and radically and sincerely examining my own motivation, I find it comes up short. I find that my own motivation is not to be here for God, but to try to have my life improved, with fewer problems, so that I could live in a state of PAGL, using Metapsychiatric language. I am really trying to improve my own life in the world.

Dr. Hora: Yes, that is what the other student wanted. She wanted to improve her life by eliminating the pain from the ankle. Most people go through this phase of hoping to use spiritual insights to better themselves in this world as human persons.

Student: I guess my question is, "What is it that keeps us there when you tell us so many times that it is futile?"

Dr. Hora: Some people make very little progress because they are too happy. They don't suffer enough.

Student: If I hadn't twisted my foot I would have gone on...

Dr. Hora: Merrily.

Student: Yes, until another accident happened, because I wasn't aware of anything except feeling good. So that's what you mean when you say that if things are going too well with someone, it is hard to be sincere.

Dr. Hora: Of course. There is an episode in the Bible where Jesus healed a man. What was wrong with him? He may have been paralyzed for a few years, and Jesus healed him. The next day he was walking on the seashore and met this guy whom he had healed, and said, "Look, you are healed." And the man said, "Yes, I feel wonderful," and Jesus said to him "Sin no more, lest a worse thing comes to you." (John 5:14) If we don't get healed of the very meaning that gave rise to that experience, then we are ready to make another mistake. Usually suffering gets worse and worse and worse until we become so desperate that we become radically sincere.

Student: Isn't the meaning always that we see ourselves as persons?

Dr. Hora: Yes, but we have to be specific. We cannot just lay down this nice cushiony saying and from now on, every time I have a problem, I know what I have to say. I have this problem because I see myself as a person.

Student: Obviously it will get me nowhere. But what I was

trying to say is that whether it is pride, ambition or vanity, it is always an urgent agenda of some personhood issue.

Dr. Hora: That's correct.

Student: So the need is still, somehow, to be able to turn away radically from that whole belief of being a person.

Dr. Hora: Well, before you turn away you have to turn to it, so that you completely understand the meaning of your problem. Don't run away. Just stay with it until you see that your suffering is just an expression of an erroneous idea of yourself as a human person.

Student: Even if it lasts all my life? (laughter)

Dr. Hora: We're not in a hurry.

Student: Dr. Hora, this is sort of like what the other student was saying. You say that suffering is very necessary. I am thinking of the incident in the Bible where the rich man comes and he is willing to endure suffering up to a point. He is willing to go so far. Then Jesus challenges him and tells him to sell everything and come and follow him. The man turned around and left. Now supposing that's the way life seems most of the time. You're willing to go so far, and unless you get this tremendous amount of suffering or something, you are not going to make that change. On the one hand, we do not want to invite some bad event; so when I hear you, I think, "I may not make that transition."

Dr. Hora: Okay, you are just left behind to repeat the quest. Life is a school, a school of hard knocks, and we have to learn one lesson. There is just one subject in this school: What Is God? That's all. We have to become totally acquainted with what God is, because then we find the truth of who we are and what we are, and that's the lesson. It's very simple. You can read it in a book, but you will not realize it that way.

Student: So if we are willing to face up to the meaning over and over and over again, do we discover what God is not?

Dr. Hora: We discover that we are not really interested in God; we are interested in something else. So you go to school to learn about God, and, instead of that, you are interested in something else. So you are frittering away your time. What grade would you give such a student? There are students who go to school and they are not interested in learning anything. They want to play basketball or football. There are misdirected interests. But of course, then we are lost.

Student: There is another factor. Suffering has a self-confirmatory element in it. It gives a very confused signal because you think that you really want not to suffer. But if it has a self-confirmatory element to it, it is really not true. So it is confusing because you think whether you might want to suffer, without realizing that it is not that you really want to suffer, but that you want to confirm yourself.

Dr. Hora: This is the secret meaning of masochism. There are people who feel good about feeling bad, where pain has become eroticized. So we hear of people who do all kinds of painful things, asking to be abused in many ways, and always they get a charge out of the pain that is inflicted on them. Of course, this is an extremely embarrassing problem. They will have a hard time being sincere about admitting the problem and they require guidance and liberation from this secret worshipping of pain. Sometimes we wonder how anybody can be such an idiot as to join a satanic cult where they hurt each other. There are people who are interested in such things. The world of personhood is a big zoo, with endless variations of distorted life.

3

Needs vs. Wants

Student: In the context of wanting, the Bible says that God knows what we need before we ask, that in Divine Reality there is recognition of what we need. Are all our needs different or is there one need? How does it work? That seems like a helpful idea in order to transcend wanting.

Dr. Hora: Does anyone know the answer to that interesting question?

Student: Aren't our needs individual, specific to our uniqueness as spiritual children of God?

Dr. Hora: There is a common need. In the whole universe, every creature endowed with consciousness has the need and the responsibility to come to know the truth. "And this is life eternal, that they may know thee, the only true God, and Jesus Christ, whom thou hast sent" (St. John 17:3). Humanity has a great need to know the truth and here was this Jewish rabbi by the name of Joshua, (laughter) and God said you go among these people and help them to come to know the truth. This is our common need.

Student: Is that our only need?

Dr. Hora: Yes, this is so. Now if anyone reaches the point where he really knows the truth, what more can you ask? You have everything. If you have the knowledge of the truth, you're enlightened. And what do you do then? You sit down cross-legged and smile and everything comes to you. That's all.

Student: It's wonderful the way you describe it, but it's hard to see it.

Dr. Hora: Yes, it's hard to see it but you have the great blessing of at least hearing about it. (laughter) Most people don't even have the foggiest idea of this truth. Yet it is so simple.

Student: Every time we see that we want something we can use that as a spiritual stimulus?

Dr. Hora: Of course, have you ever heard of the first principle of Metapsychiatry? What does it say? Thou shalt have no other interests before the good of God, which is spiritual blessedness. Now what's so great about spiritual blessedness? If somebody is in a condition of spiritual blessedness, what else can he want or need? He is absolutely free, absolutely perfect, absolutely intelligent, absolutely glowing and joyous and he lives forever. He will never die and he knows it. He doesn't have to go anywhere because God is present everywhere. So why run around looking for happiness when it is right under your nose? This is very strange, isn't it? We are constantly hearing about the truth. Truth is a very fantastic idea. The bible says, "You shall know the truth and the truth shall make you free." It shall make you healthy. It shall make you happy. It shall make you infinitely wealthy. It shall make you satisfied. There is nothing else left to crave or to want. You are fearless. You have no worries. You know that nothing, not even an atomic explosion, could destroy you. How is that? Is that an exaggeration?

Student: It seems that our needs will be met if we are enlightened. But is there any alternative? (laughter)

Dr. Hora: If our need is met then all needs are met. Our need is to come to know the truth.

Student: So as life unfolds and we keep that primary interest, does that take over, because the interest is so focused that we don't have to think about not wanting? I mean one does get into a kind of struggle if one focuses on wanting and not wanting.

Dr. Hora: Beautiful. This is so simple, so wonderful and so universal. What is it that interferes with achieving it? Wanting and "shoulding," right? I just mentioned to a student that there was an alcoholic who was studying Metasychiatry and he said, "The reason I drink is that there are so many liquor stores in the city." And then I said, "If there were no liquor stores at all in NewYork, you wouldn't have an alcoholic problem? Then all you have to do is to throw bombs to destroy the liquor stores. Then you wouldn't have any problem." Is that so? Certainly not, because then he would think about what should be, what shouldn't be, what I want, and what I don't want. Now what makes us so stupid? Everybody is constantly thinking about what they want and what they don't want, and what should be and what shouldn't be. I remember a husband whose favorite saying to his wife was, "If only you would change, I would be all right." So we have all these ideas. We arrive at these ideas by judging by appearances. And that's the basic problem. Jesus said to judge not by appearances. If we judge by appearance we have all kinds of invalid ideas occurring and of course we are cut off from what we really need. Everybody has this one need. And there is only one need.

Student: That's beautiful; it simplifies it.

Dr. Hora: Whether you are an addict or a Russian or this or that, you only have one need. It's the same need for everybody. That's why racism doesn't make any sense. The blacks have the same need, the whites have the same need, the yellows have... the need is universal and unique, one.

Student: What about the need to eat? What about the need to sleep?

Dr. Hora: What about? What did Jesus say to "the what about?"

Student: Take no thought about what we should wear or what we should eat...

Dr. Hora: Seek ye first the consciousness of divine reality and all these things shall be added onto you.

Student: So it does seem that God has taken care of all our needs, like shelter and food. We just must be aware that it comes from God.

Dr. Hora: Once the disciples of Jesus brought some food to him and said, "Master, here is some food; you haven't eaten all day; will you eat?" Jesus answered that he had food to eat that the disciple didn't know of. Once he hadn't eaten for forty days, and what did he say? "My meat is to do the will of him that sent me." (John 4:34) So he knew the truth; he had no need for drinking water or eating food; none of these things were important to him, and whenever something was needed, it appeared.

Student: He expressed some concern for the homeless.

Dr. Hora: Oh yes. What did he say about the homeless?

Student: They'll always be with us.

Dr. Hora: No. About the homeless he said this: "Birds have nests, foxes have holes, but the son of man has no place to lay his head." Was he complaining? (laughter)

Student: He got caught up in the sense that we ought to be doing something for other people—the social justice issue. What does Metapsychiatry say about that sort of thing?

Dr. Hora: Metapsychiatry has a wonderful solution for every problem. What do you think? Metapsychiatry never does anything. If there is a problem, we don't fix the problem. What do we do when we are confronted with a problem? We pray. Normal people say this shouldn't be and we have to fix it. But Metapsychiatry says that this isn't. Perfect universe is and prayer is the acknowledgment of the perfection of divine reality. Wherever phenomena appear disquieting and people are anxious and suffer and are fearful and they try to fix everything, it is never fixed. The only remedy to the ills of the world is the conscious awareness of the perfection of the universe, which already is and always was and always will be. Now, our knowledge is not sufficient to immediately see the disappearance of New York City's problems, but on individual levels we see marvelous changes taking place in peoples' lives when they stop thinking about what shouldn't be and focus their attention on what already is. To this effect there has been written a second principle of Metapsychiatry. Have we ever heard of it? How does it go?

Students and Dr. Hora recite: "Take no thought for what should be or shouldn't be; seek ye first to know the good of God which already is."

Dr. Hora: Okay? So whenever we are confronted with something, we pray with the help of the second principle and we see changes happening. Not on a large scale, because we don't have that amount of knowledge, but on an individual scale we see that this is so.

Student: If it's the truth and we can see it on an individual level, what knowledge is necessary? Is it the same knowledge?

Dr. Hora: This is a very good question and Jesus somehow hinted at it. He said, "He that believeth on me, the works that I do shall he do also; and greater works than these shall he do; because I go unto my Father." (John 14:12) How could anybody do greater works than this fantastic guy? And what did he mean? Greater works than these shall ye do, for I go unto my Father. The answer offers itself that he may have hinted at the fact of a collective knowledge of the truth. If one individual can know the truth and see remarkable healings and changes occurring, then a collective of a large number of individuals who can join knowing the truth, might result in who knows what—tremendous blessings in the world. To this effect, people in various parts of the world form groups and schools and religious groups and try to know the truth collectively, for greater power. Unfortunately they have not succeeded in synchronizing their knowledge of the truth. Because what happens when larger numbers of sincere seekers of the truth come together in order to pray? We see that many churches and denominations and all kinds of religious groups come together to pray for the world but we don't see any spectacular results from that. The only explanation for this is that while they do pray they do not pray with sufficient understanding. Because there are not too many enlightened individuals in the world yet, and throughout history they were only scattered here and there. When people who came together to try to pray, their prayers were not effective. There was a guy on television the other day, a Southern Baptist; who has 30 million adherents to his religion. And he got up in front of them and said, "God doesn't listen to Jewish prayer. Why? Because they rejected Jesus." It's a personal affair. Okay, so here was a man who is religious, but doesn't really understand that the truth is not personal or denominational. Suppose there is this collective desire to pray for the world but the people don't really understand. Then even if 10,000 well meaning individuals were to pray, it would have no effect whatsoever.

Student: Because their prayers are asking for things?

Dr. Hora: Sure, they are asking and telling; everybody has his or her own personal misconceptions. There are collective misconceptions and individual misconceptions. But prayer is not effective unless it is according to the way Jesus specified it. He said, "God is Spirit and they that worship him must worship him in spirit and in truth." (John 4:24) But who has already sufficiently advanced on this path to worship God in spirit? Most of the world worships God in ceremonies and in words, pretty words, sometimes in singing, and even in jiving. (laughter) But there are very few people, relatively speaking, who can worship God in spirit and in truth, as Jesus specified it. Why did he say this in this particular way? What is this, in spirit and in truth? What did he mean? What was his reason for saying it this way?

Student: Well, ceremonies at the time were outward in form.

Dr. Hora: Even so today. But what does it mean: "in spirit and in truth."

Student: It's the third step that you've been describing to enlightenment: God as man. If you have reached that level of oneness, you are worshiping in spirit and in truth.

Dr. Hora: Yes, indeed. If we don't understand that we are spiritual beings made of the same stuff that God is, then we don't have the truth and we cannot effectively pray. In order to pray effectively we have to understand that reality is God, and that man and his Creator are made of the stuff which is spirit. And to the extent that this is understood the truth is known. Now if there were a group like this, even a small group and if every one of us knew this who knows what would happen? Right, the truth might become more and more widely known as we progress. But collectively we don't know how to pray and that's the problem.

Student: You've never explained the meaning of the statement that man has no place to lay his head.

Dr. Hora: Yes. Foxes have holes, birds have nests but the son of man has no place to lay his head. He was hinting at the fact that he was not one of these creatures. He was of a higher order. He didn't really mean a bed or a hole, you see. He hardly ever wore any shoes. And he could walk on water; he could transport himself over distances instantaneously; he could walk into a room through a closed door. What did he mean by saying that the son of man has no place to lay his head?

Student: He didn't really mean himself?

Dr. Hora: Yes, of course. Interchangeably he called himself the son of God or the son of man, indicating that he is both at the same time. He didn't need to have a place to lay his head. Okay, so the more people learn how to pray, to reach the level of enlightenment, where prayer becomes knowledge of the spiritual truth, the better the world will be. For the time being it seems to be going from bad to worse. There is so much ignorance in the world, so many tragedies, so many frightening things. That's the way the cookie crumbles. The human individual has to become enlightened in order to pray effectively. But as we approach that level of enlightenment, the word prayer is not enough anymore. Instead of prayer we can say that knowing, that right knowing is the ultimate prayer. So if you know the truth there is nothing to pray for anymore, right?

Prayer has been imbued with the idea of begging. Man has to beg for everything and God is the richest man in the United States so we can beg him to give us what we want. Right? So in Metapsychiatry we learn to abandon the idea of petitionary prayer. In all religions there is petitionary prayer, man begging God. But we don't beg in order to get recognition; instead, since we want to have self respect even in the face of God, we call prayer right knowing. "This is life eternal, that they might know thee the only true God, and Jesus Christ, whom thou hast sent." (John: 17-3) If we understand that prayer is right knowing, then it is easier to stop thinking about what should be or what shouldn't be, or what we want or what we don't want.

There is a demonstration going on in the street; somebody, perhaps union people, are striking. Now even the doctors are on strike. They go in the streets with placards and one of them cries out, "What do we want?" and the others call out, "More money." It's very funny to watch. Well that's life.

Student: I have another question. Can the subconscious subvert the conscious? For instance, sometimes I'm understanding Metapsychiatry, and then I wake up from a dream that is not a happy one or I think of something I did before and I regret it. The state of peace isn't constant. Now is there any point of thinking in terms of the subconscious? What is the next step?

Dr. Hora: Well, as you know the subconscious is a psychoanalytic invention that says we have to struggle against certain thoughts which we are not fully aware of. And these thoughts sometimes come to torment us either during the day or at night when we are trying to sleep, and they torment us because they are pressing for conscious acknowledgment. So we eagerly look at our dreams and ask what each dream is trying to tell us about our secret thoughts. Very often we develop certain unacceptable thoughts during the day or from our past and they can torment us and come up in the form of physical symptoms, or disturbances in our social life, or economic problems, or other kinds of things. So the great value of the two intelligent questions is that when we confront these mental phenomena with the question, "What is the meaning of what seems to be?" and we are inspired and suddenly realize the answer to this question, then we know what the so-called unconscious or subconscious was harboring. It invariably turns out to be some thought that we would rather not be aware of. Inquiring about the meaning is extremely helpful. The Freudian method aimed at the same thing, in a way, when Freud devised the method of free association. It involves going at random through our thoughts with the hope that the blind chicken will find the kernel. But we have a method which is much more effective if it's approached with a sense of radical sincerity and a willingness to be embarrassed about it.

Student: I just have to keep persevering with that question; it's not a quick fix.

Dr. Hora: Sometimes we become aware of it quickly and sometimes we have to wait; it depends upon how squeamish we are. (chuckle)

Student: This question seems to be similar. Last week there were two articles in the newspaper that seemed to be dealing with the physiology of the brain. One article described an x-ray photograph of the mind in the process of retrieving a word. In the other article there was a review of a book in which the doctor had apparently, very elaborately, laid out what parts of the brain do what. It went to an extreme to describe how we think there's something in there controlling and modulating our thoughts. Yet, what was interesting was that all the other scientists have always fallen back on the soul or what we call consciousness because there must be an organizing principle. This person said, "No, no, there's no organizing principle." But when the scientists all get together they conflict. For some reason psychology and physio-neurology...and this is of concern to me and makes a question come up. I was wondering if perhaps science will just accept things to the point...

Dr. Hora: To what point?

Student: Organizing the whole.

Dr. Hora: There was a very wise doctor who said, they know more and more about less and less until they find out that they know everything about nothing. This is called reductionism. Reductionism has been a trend in scientific research for years, and everything tends toward it; the attempt is to reduce everything to the molecular, to the atomic, and sub-atomic level and explain life in terms of *reductio ad absurdum*. Of course it doesn't explain anything. It observes certain phenomena, in terms of larger scale or smaller phenomena, which are appearances, but they don't explain life, and such descriptions have absolutely no value. It's interesting, of course. Neuro-physiology is interesting, but it can never really explain life because it leaves God out of his own creation.

Student: I was thinking that it almost seems like a 1990s version of Darwin and how Darwin's theories evolved to threaten....and

Dr. Hora: These aren't threatening anymore; these are ridiculous. They don't explain, they describe phenomena. Describing a phenomenon doesn't explain it.

Student: I guess it is the determination of these people to say that there isn't...

Dr. Hora: There is no God. Yes, of course. Well it's almost as bad as saying that God is Jewish or Arabic. Whether you deny the existence of God or misinterpret the existence of God it's the same because you deprive yourself of the possibility of salvation through enlightenment. What good is that? So you've given an explanation which is reductionistic and when you have a bellyache you don't know where to go.

Student: In the past you've spoken of life as non-dimensional. I understand that, and that as we are transparencies, that we've never really seen somebody else. There seems to be this thing in human existence. We're so certain... We're looking for something so that we can say this is it. We're looking for something dimensional as an explanation.

Dr. Hora: Dimensional, yes. Be it ever so tiny, as long as it has dimensions it's respectable because it's material. In accepted atomic research they've reached a point where they see subatomic particles as corpuscular, material little balls. And as they watched these little balls, suddenly they would disappear and in place of them waves would appear. They lost their dimensionality and they were just phenomena. So when you go far enough you will know everything about nothing or nothing about everything. There is no other solution. There was a lady in Los Angeles at a church meeting and they were discussing bilingual religious services in that church; and this lady got up and said, "Why do we need bilingual services? If English was good enough for Jesus....." (laughter) It's folk wisdom.

Student: To come back to the idea of collective spirit, knowing?

Dr. Hora: Collective knowing of the truth. ...

Student: Collective knowing of the truth can be potentiating.

Dr. Hora: Yes, potentiation is a good word. I have observed different monks pray and there is an absurdity where they whirl around the prayer-wheels and this is considered prayer for them. But then I've seen on television, different monks who are more serious students of the truth; they were humming in very deep voices, continuous humming collectively so they were synchronized; they were all humming on a certain wave length. I asked myself, "What kind of meditation could this be?" There is a collective humming and every participant is tuned in literally on the same wave length. I didn't understand. Nobody explained what this humming means, but I imagine that it is one attempt of collective prayer where concepts are eliminated. No conceptual attempt at prayer, but actually, sort of immersing consciousness into a collective wave length. Maybe that is one form that approximates the prayer of right knowing. I have not seen what they have accomplished. But there is a beautiful exhibit at the IBM Center about Tibetan Art that is mind-boggling. That these people, hundreds of years ago, were able to produce under religious fervor this kind of art, such amazing things! But there's much we don't understand about these cultures. Anyway there is the power of the truth and the spirit that throughout the history of mankind has manifested itself through individuals in the miraculous healings or artistic expression or opera stars.

Student: Would that humming, all that humming together create an emptiness?

Dr. Hora: I really don't know. But it was very fascinating.

Student: At the IBM exhibit there was a film of them making this huge sand painting for three months, doing it quietly, and when they were all through, they scraped it together, put it into bottles and threw it away. And I interpreted it as meaning...that

Dr. Hora: Uselessness.

Student: That life was meaningless. They showed them doing it.

Dr. Hora: Did they explain?

Student: They don't speak very well.

Dr. Hora: No, they spoke English. But they also do sand paintings in person. They are very simple and they said that their mission was wisdom and compassion.

Student: The meaning is not uselessness, but impermanence. The meaning of going to great length of making the sand mandala and destroying it is to show the impermanence of life.

Student: How do you evaluate what happens in these groups? It seems that at the end of the session, a lot of errors have been replaced in everyone's consciousness by truth and it seems that that would help.

Dr. Hora: That would be nice. If you leave here and are reached with love, a loving outlook on life, then it would be a useful session. Someone stopped the group on the street in front of the house and asked, "Is this a charm school?" (laughter) Yes, the quality of love is a very good indicator whether we are responding to the truth or not. It is highly desirable to be uplifting, and to see life more in the context of divine love, non-conditional benevolence. When Buddhists speak about wisdom and compassion, their idea of compassion is benevolence. We have a different definition of compassion. We speak about love-intelligence. They speak about wisdom and compassion. But it's very similar. There is no theological rift between them. Do we still remember the definition of perfect love, yes? Non-personal, non-conditional benevolence. It helps to know this. Love is a force. Throughout the world you see love destroying people. It's very strange. How does love destroy people?

Student: It's conditional.

Dr. Hora: Because it's conditional. If you love conditionally, you can drive somebody crazy. Everybody is very eager to be loved. Everybody wants to be loved and if this love that you crave has strings attached to it, which it always has, then you become entrapped in a certain way of thinking and behaving and it can become very bad. So human love is dangerous, creating an outright conflict. Believe it or not. But the understanding of perfect love, as the bible puts it, "Perfect love casteth out fear," (John 4:18) is liberating. If you ask somebody, "What does the bible mean by perfect love?" the answer will most often be unselfish love. That's what most people will say. The bible speaks about unselfish love. Now what do you think? Is there such a thing?

Student: If you transcend the idea that you're a person, wouldn't that be synonymous with being unselfish?

Dr. Hora: No. Selflessness. Sometimes people speak of selflessness which is very close to perfect love.

Student: Unselfish love is being here for others.

Dr. Hora: Right, it's being here for others. In selfish love, you are here for yourself, while unselfish love is being here for others so that you can benefit from thinking of yourself as loving...(laughter) It's part of the screwed up human condition.

Student: It's difficult to understand love impersonally.

Dr. Hora: Non-personally. Well that's what we have arrived at: this realization that perfect love must be non-personal because it's divine and non-conditional. There are no strings attached. It is benevolent. Nothing mushy about it. It's benevolent and real. That's perfect love.

4

Existential Speaking

Student: Dr. Hora, I am still unable to shake this habit of talking about myself with others, especially at work, and it always seems to get me in trouble.

Dr. Hora: Right.

Student: I guess I don't understand something well enough, something that would tell me to stop when I start.

Dr. Hora: What do you like to say about yourself? How handsome you are? (laughter)

Student: People ask questions. They say, "What are you doing tonight?" or "What are you doing this weekend?"

Dr. Hora: There's nothing wrong with speaking about that.

Student: Then they ask who was your date or the party you attended.

Dr. Hora: "my date was a fig" (laughter)

Student: Very sweet.

Student: It's difficult not to answer.

Dr Hora: Well if you don't answer, then you're snubbing somebody. You have to answer in such a way that you are issue oriented, not self-oriented. In the realm of reality, there is neither self nor other; there is only is. Is you is?

Student: How does that apply to life, because the questions brought up seem harmless?

Dr. Hora: The questions are harmless; it's the answers that are not. (laughter)

Student: Well, what's the error if he or she asks about a date he had last night, and he says it was fine; we did this or that, and we keep it on that light level. What's wrong with that?

Dr. Hora: Nothing, Absolutely nothing. You're talking about yesterday which was a day. You're not talking about yourself. You don't have to say "I felt like this or I felt like that." Every day has something interesting, right?

Student: So if we don't bring it down to the level of feeling or opinions or praise or blaming..

Dr. Hora: Right... relationships, personal success, failure. The question was "How was the day?" "The day was raining."

Student: What if she asks, "Was she good-looking?" That's a personal question.

Dr. Hora: The problem is talking about oneself. It's interesting to watch these talk shows on television. Most people who stand up to say something want to talk about themselves. They don't talk to the issue anymore, but they use the issue to draw attention to themselves. That's the normal way to be: egotistical and unenlightened. And then, of course, nobody wants to let him go on, so others jump in to stop him from talking about himself, because they want to talk about themselves. And what you have in these situations are several people talking at the same time and nobody understands anything, right? This becomes the phenomenon of simultaneously talking. This comedian, Jackie Mason, has the same problem on his TV show; everybody jumps in and doesn't let each other talk and he tries to control it, and the harder he tries to control it the worse the situation gets until he gets fed up, turns around and walks away. Have you seen it? That's his only solution. First he tries to suppress it and that doesn't work so he walks away and he comes back later.

Student: So the response can either have an element of wanting to confirm ourselves as a certain kind of individual or it could address the issue of the event itself.

Dr. Hora: In a non-personal way, non self-referential way, issues can be discussed, clarified, explained and there would be no clashing of opinions. This traffic jam wouldn't occur if you knew how to speak to issues.

Student: So if someone asked you where you went and you said we went to this restaurant and then you said the food's good there. Is that okay?

Dr. Hora: Did they ask you about the food?

Student: They didn't ask that; you just offered that and that's bringing in…
Dr. Hora: That's gratuitous; it means, "I did eat there, I can

afford this and I feel good about the food." It already intro-
duces the personal element. If they ask you about the food,
you could say, "lousy." (laughter) That would bring an end to
the conversation, because there's nothing to brag about.

Student: Do we invite these questions?

Dr. Hora: Certainly. The more self-confirmatory we are the
more we invite these situations. And people do not want to
hear you talk about yourself. They want to hear you talk about
them. It is very troublesome to talk about ourselves. We invite
a great deal of hostility and provocation; it's remarkable how
quickly people can become incensed with each other over un-
important issues if they are self-confirmatory. Even in their
thoughts. Thoughts are also provocative. Jesus used to say
"verily, verily, I say unto you." What could be more self-confirmatory than that? Right? And, indeed, people took exception
to this manner of talking. And they said, "your words are not
true, because you're bearing record of yourself." So what did he
say? He said, "but I, I am an exception." How is it that he could
talk about himself and that's all right and nobody else can talk
about himself without that getting him into trouble?

Student: He said, "I and my father are one and it is not I that
speaketh but the father within me."

Dr. Hora: He said something like that...

Student: "I know where I come from and whither I go."

Dr. Hora: "and ye don't know." You see, after you become
enlightened, then you can brag. (laughter)
Student: Is all talking about ourselves bragging, whether it's

positive or negative?

Dr. Hora: Self-confirmatory ideation is just bragging. That's all. There are two kinds of bragging. There is positive bragging and negative bragging, yes? Some people are positive braggers and some people are negative braggers. Now, if Jesus said, "I know where I came from," so what gives him the right to talk about himself, just because he knew where he came from? It's as if I would say, "Well I came from Czechoslovakia, so it's all right for me to talk about myself."

Student: It meant that he knew his true identity.

Dr. Hora: He knew his true identity. What was that?

Student: It was as a child of God, an instrument of God; he was speaking in a way to express spiritual values and his understanding of God's ideas.

Dr. Hora: He also knew that God was talking through him. All the thoughts that he expressed were constantly flowing into his consciousness from the Divine Mind and that's highly desirable. If you understand that, then you have no right to open your mouth unless God is pushing you. Then it's okay. We say here that communication is from God to man. And there aren't too many people who can talk from that perspective; as the spirit moves them, they speak. Such communication is valid and it is good; it is intelligent and it is comforting. Whereas human communication, person to person, is always disturbing. Even if it is positive it is still disturbing. Because person to person is not communication; it is manipulation. One individual cannot say anything to another individual without there being a hidden motive behind it. They are so screwed up that such talk is always influencing, manipulating and wanting something or not wanting something.

Student: What about goodwill?

Dr. Hora: Goodwill? That's nice. Here you see that there are people who are called nice. Nice people express personal goodwill, and it always turns out to be a lie. As St. Paul said, "All men are liars." So, if you are nice, you're lying and manipulating so that people should like you, right? So you cannot be nice. God is love, which is non-conditional benevolence. Look at what parents do to their children with the best of intentions. They're nice to their children. They want to love their children. But what is parental love. It is conditional. Therefore, it is harmful.

Student: Then the purest motivation is perfect love.

Dr. Hora: Sure.

Student: Built into the definition of perfect love is benevolence.

Dr. Hora: Yes, but what kind?

Student: That was my question.

Dr. Hora: Nonpersonal benevolence. Okay, you are being nice. You are being helpful. You are being a comforter and it's nothing because it's being done by a person. A person is trying to be good. Now how can a person be good if there is no such thing as a person? So, if you see a person who is being

Existential Speaking

good, the Zen master said, "slay him." What they say is, "If you meet the Buddha on the way slay him." Because there are many people who pretend to be buddhas. And they may believe it, sincerely, though they are just lying. They are insincere. They are phony. It is not real. It is nauseating when there is somebody trying to pretend to be nice.

Student: One time where I work, we had a problem with communications, and things weren't going right. So what they did was to bring in Dale Carnegie trainers, and they trained 50 people at a time. And during meetings, things were going pretty good but after about a year things went back to the way they were before. There was a lot of good manipulating, even better manipulating towards the end. But we believe that we have to have interpersonal communication. We cannot survive as a corporation if we cannot relate to people, to find out what their problems are and to try to sell the product.

Dr. Hora: Yes.

Student: So my question is, "how can we get away from that mode of being and still survive as a corporation?"

Dr. Hora: This is not a relevant question. Who gives a damn about the corporation? We're talking about reality. Is a corporation a reality? Let's ask an expert on corporations. Is a corporation a reality?

Student: No, it's an idea.

Dr. Hora: It's a construct. It starts as a mental construct; somebody puts together these ideas and then tries to make it work. You don't find too many corporation presidents who are enlightened or are interested in spiritual reality or anything. This is the world. So if you are in the world you are naturally drawn into this world of artificiality, interaction, and self-confirmation. It is necessary. But we are not talking about the world. We are talking about overcoming the world. Why bother with overcoming the world? Why not be, as the psychologists say, a well adjusted person. This is the idea of psychology. You get well adjusted to the world. As the rabbi said, it's not forbidden. It's okay.

Student: Well, to be well adjusted... there's no freedom in that; it's just behavior.

Dr. Hora: Well, who gives a damn about freedom if you make a lot of money? Isn't that what will give you freedom? Isn't money good?

Student: Only if it's a byproduct of love.

Dr. Hora: We are always running into the brick wall of the world. We have to live in the world with all its complexities and lack of authenticity. Everything in the world is phony and insincere and yet we are in it. In order to economically and socially survive we have to be well adjusted. If you want to live in Greenwich Village you have to be gay or become an outsider. A well adjusted person conforms to the prevailing values of a particular culture. This is necessary as long as our aspirations are just for being in the world. What Jesus said was that if you are in the world you will have tribulations. No matter how adjusted you are you are going to run into trouble. So, the prophet who wrote the 91st psalm, says, "Because thou hast made the LORD, which is my refuge, even the most High, thy habitation; there shall no evil befall thee, neither shall any plague come nigh thy dwelling. For he shall give his angels charge over thee, to keep thee in all thy ways. They shall bear thee up in their hands, lest thou dash thy foot against a stone." (Ps. 91:9-12) Now what was he talking about?

Student: Safety.

Dr. Hora: He was talking about overcoming the world by seeking to dwell in the secret place of the most high or under the shadow of the almighty. This happens if we make the Lord our habitation, which means that we see ourselves mentally involved in the good of God always. And the good of God is more important to us than golf or sports or clothes or membership in clubs or anything. The mind must be constantly preoccupied with the good of God, divine reality. That is the only way that we can be spared unpleasant surprises. Everybody has unpleasant surprises. The other day I was listening to Robert Schuller. You know he is a California preacher, a very well known man, a talented man. His sermon was about how terrible it is that we run into surprises in life. We are constantly running into some unexpected surprises. The more we are out of it, the worse the surprises are. The Bible says that no evil shall befall thee if you dwell in the secret place of the most high. Now, who has not experienced unpleasant surprises in his life? Everybody. And if you look for the meaning of that surprise, you will find that you have strayed from your dwelling place. Because there are so many distractions, so seductive, so provocative, that we constantly keep losing our focus on God.

Student: Dr. Hora, talking about dwelling place, I have a

noise problem in my apartment. My apartment is not quiet. When I manage to become peaceful the noise goes away. When I listen it comes back; it's just torture.

Dr. Hora: We start by thanking God that you are thrown into a situation that you are forced to dwell in the secret place of the most high.

Student: But the part that confuses me is that when it's the neighbor, I see that loving thoughts are needed. And then when it's the boiler noise I just feel that it's hard to... (laughter) Is it the same, even though...

Dr. Hora: Yes, everything is the same, the boiler or the neighbor, the cats and the dogs and the spouses. Everything we experience in life depends on whether or not we dwell in the secret place of the most high. It is a fantastic thing.

Student: The 91st Psalm and the first principle seem to be saying the same thing.

Dr. Hora: Yes. But most of the time we think that these are just prayers. These are not just prayers; they are pointers to overcoming the world. What are we overcoming when we are really interested in overcoming the world? Whatever we cherish, whatever we hate and whatever we fear is the world, and it is outside of the House of the Lord, outside of our dwelling place. And who is there that doesn't cherish things, who doesn't hate things, and who is not afraid? Most everybody has this problem. And the Bible says, you have to dwell in the secret place of the most high. In other words, your consciousness has to be constantly aware that reality is spiritual and you dwell in the secret place of the most high. It's secret because most people don't understand it. We cannot cherish anything, we cannot be afraid of anything, and certainly we cannot hate absolutely anything. We cannot even hate crime or injustice or misery, "Because thou hast made the Lord, which is my refuge, even the most High, thy habitation; there shall no evil befall thee, neither shall any plague come nigh thy dwelling." So whenever we run into unpleasant situations by surprise or by belief in its inevitability we have to quickly come back into this dwelling place where God dwells, and we must consciously seek to dwell in that place only. The worst thing I think is the cherishing. There are so many things to cherish in life: good food, fancy clothes, friends, enemies. We always cherish things, and when we cherish something we are not dwelling in God; we are apart from God. And then all kinds of things can happen.

Student: Can we cherish God?

Dr. Hora: You have to cherish God, yes. Cherishing God means that we do not allow anything else to captivate our attention. An interesting thing happens when we find ourselves in trouble and we recognize that we have invited this trouble through diverting our attention from the secret place. Then we say, "I can come back quickly," and whenever we are sincere about it, a healing takes place. The trouble which befell us is suddenly dissolved and we are set free of its consequences. So it is a tremendous blessing to know the 91st Psalm and to understand it existentially: that it refers to our mode of being-in-the-world.

Student: Is cherishing and attachment the same thing?

Dr. Hora: Yes. Cherishing is attachment; hating is involvement. And of course, you know that when we are afraid we cannot let go of the thought from which we would like to escape. All these three aspects of the human experience are universal in everybody's life, but most people don't know what is hurting them and how to escape from it. Because reciting the words of the 91st psalm isn't going to do the trick. But immediately, that's what Heidegger meant when he said, "gelassenheit du den denken." Did you get it?

Student: I couldn't get the first part. (laughter)

Dr. Hora: **Gelassenheit du den denken.** Well, he believed that if you cherish something, and you remind yourself not to cherish it and just distance yourself from what you're cherishing, this will help. It will help, but not completely. For instance, if a Honda car is very precious to you, right, or some car, or something is precious to you and you keep thinking about it and you're hooked on it; as long as you're hooked on it, you're away from God and all kinds of things can happen. So Heidegger says, all right, you need a car, you drive a car, but don't get hooked on a car; just let it be. And Meister Eckhart, was said to have said, "Let go and let be." Don't sell your car. You need to use it, but don't make a federal case out of it. Right? The same way: **gelassenheit du den denken.** When we speak about watching television and we say that you have to watch with disinterest, that's the same thing. But it is not enough. You also have to know what you are about: that you're protecting yourself from the temptation of getting hooked on something. It can be a thing, a person, a place, an idea, money, or anything that's too important to you. You can get into trouble. I just heard on the radio that a 10 year old girl disappeared; someone snatched her away. When parents cherish their children, that is also dangerous.

Student: If we cherish an idea....?

Dr. Hora: That's what it is. If you cherish an idea you are cherishing your own brain, your intellect. We can appreciate ideas, but we must not get hooked on anything, except that we must know that we are here for God, and God must be our dwelling place. You see, whatever we dwell on mentally is our dwelling place. You can live in a palace or a beautiful apartment. But if you are not hooked on it it's all right; it's *gelassenheit*; it's letting it be. Our devotion must always be to the presence of God.

Student: Is the test of our freedom from unhealthy attachment that you can leave it anytime?

Dr. Hora: Yes. That's the test. You watch television, but you turn it off. It's no big deal. You turn it on. You turn it off. You don't have to tear yourself away. Some people get hooked on the pictures and can't turn themselves away. It is like with everything else: we are here for God, and unless we learn how to live that way life is always full of unpleasant surprises.

Student: So if we understand the 91st psalm, back to what the student asked earlier, then we can engage in a conversation. But if we are dwelling in God consciousness, then we will be able to address the issue.

Dr. Hora: Of course, in the final analysis whenever we are hooked on it we are involved with self-confirmation. "No evil shall befall thee, neither shall any plague come nigh thy dwelling." Some years ago, one of our students went to a synagogue. And he heard the rabbi giving a sermon against the 91st psalm. He was berating this psalm.

Student: On what basis?

Dr. Hora: I don't know. It's unbelievable. It's from the Old Testament. It's hard to believe.

Student: You spoke about unpleasant surprises. We experienced something that happened on Christmas Day. Someone we knew was killed in a fire (in New Jersey) and the whole family is destroyed. That has nothing to do with me, does it? It's an unpleasant surprise.

Dr. Hora: It has to do with the Christmas spirit. What is the Christmas spirit? Greed, possessiveness, preoccupation with gifts and personal relationships. After Christmas the place is almost empty. People get sick left and right. They get colds, get the flu, and have accidents. All kinds of things happen to people on holidays and Christmas is one of the most dangerous holidays of the year. Because it is so hyped up in everybody's mind: what will I get? How many cards will I receive in the mail? Will the neighbors notice that I am getting Christmas cards? You see, we get seduced by the general insanity involved in celebrating holidays. Many tragic events happen much more during holidays than otherwise. Holidays are dangerous times. We have to celebrate with sincere disinterest.

Student: For me, celebrating is like the noosphere, I can sense this craziness going on and that scares me.

Dr. Hora: But it's no excuse. The Bible says, since you have taken up the study of Metapsychiatry, thou hast no excuse. You are beholden to God not to be distracted from his presence, just because it is a holiday. God doesn't take holidays. Did you know that? He never goes for a vacation. In Him we live and move and have our being and we must be conscious of this. We have to be in this consciously, because if we get hooked on things, the tinsel of the world, we are not dwelling in God and that's where we are exposed to danger, unexpected danger. Possessiveness is a very troublesome habit of thought. If you are inclined to be possessive of someone or something then you are hooked on that and then you are not in your dwelling place. So when we are possessive we are inviting all kinds of troublesome experience.

Student: One thing that is troublesome to me is, when you're with another individual and you want to show consideration and it seems appropriate. And then, in a short time, I am finding that it's interpreted as the other person can lead the way or just do anything they want, and then I'm resentful. Now this is a very human level and I know it. Is there a way when you're with another to be with God and to be considerate. I see that what's happening is no good.

Dr. Hora: Well, first, you have to learn to speak. For instance, you say, you want to show consideration. Now what kind of a sentence is that? What does it say? You want to show consideration.

Student: It's operational.

Dr. Hora: It's operational, it's phony, and it's nice. It's manipulative. You're out of it. You're not being considerate. Being considerate is a form of love and it's a godly way to be, but to show consideration, you see, this is manipulation. This has nothing to do with God. We don't do that. It's not nice to do these things. We have to be authentically spiritual, here for God. God is love, God is truth. God is authenticity. God is genuineness. God is forthrightness. We don't just show it. We are it. There is so much insincerity in the world. They think they have to show it to make impressions. We're not in God: we're on Broadway or in Hollywood. We have to be careful of our words and our syntax because there is a lot hidden in it. You want to show consideration: if you show consideration somebody else will show you a fist in your nose.

Student: You're saying to be careful with your words. Isn't our motivation revealed by our words?

Dr. Hora: Well, it's ignorance. It's with the best of intentions. We don't understand the difference between being considerate and showing consideration. There are many such phrases which betray our ignorance of forthright living. When we are here for God and we live and move and have our being in God, then our language changes. Phrases which we previously used without much examination become changed. Perhaps from now on, you will never say, "I want to show consideration." So we learn to talk using right language. Now the Bible says "They shall [learn to] speak with new tongues. (Mark 16:17) The evangelists think that when a congregant is moved to talk nonsense that this is the new tongue. Psychiatrists call this glossolalia and consider it a symptom of schizophrenia. There are people in institutions who constantly wag their tongues at each other and make such noises that in the churches are considered high spirituality. Let's not get hooked on glossolalia. There are sincere Christians who believe because they know how to do this that somehow they have been specially blessed by God. It's interesting that some of them pride themselves on being able to get up in church and make these noises. And then somebody else will get up and say, "I understand what he is saying; I can translate it; I can interpret it." So now we have two people confirming themselves as spiritual giants.

5

Conundrum of Giving and Getting

Dr. Hora: In Pasadena, California, there is a church, and a college called Ambassador College. This church is a very successful church; it is known worldwide and is held in high esteem by religious people. The head of this religious movement was an interesting man who had his own theory about life. He believed in it very strongly and built up a tremendous source of revenue from it. He became a multi-millionaire. The church had jet planes and palaces in various places. It is called the Worldwide Church of God. If you listen to the television on Sunday mornings, they still have a program, and they have very intelligent religious lectures. And this man had a very simple explanation of religion and the cure of all problems in the world. He flew to China and to Russia. Everywhere he was welcomed and held in high esteem, and people listened to his lectures. And the lectures were always the same. He said the trouble with the world is that everybody wants to get and nobody wants to give. And all the difficulties come from this idea that the important thing is to get. Therefore, what we have to do is to change our thinking from get to give. And people took to this like thirsty people to fresh water. It was very nice, so simple, so good. Who could object to this? And money came pouring in. Have you ever seen this Pasadena Church? It has absolutely, fantastically, beautiful buildings and auditoriums and school equipment. It's a functioning organization based on this simple idea that all you have to do is switch from a desire to get to a desire to give. Yes? And it seems to work. It's wonderful. It's almost just as good as winning friends and influencing people! People go for these simple things because it's easy. And they gather together. And of course they are very intelligent, highly educated people who are in charge now. The founder of the church died about two years ago, but it's still thriving. Now the amazing thing is that it's a fallacy and yet it works because to give or to get is the same. No wonder it works, because if you are giving, you are confirming yourself; if you are getting, you are also confirming yourself. You can't lose.

I was following this development for a few years and watching it go on. Of course, they had their crisis. The old man had a son who was also preaching, but he was at the same time womanizing around, and the father got very mad and expelled him from the church. He disenfranchised his own son and took in some other people. At one point they had some difficulty with the IRS but they had some clever lawyers who arranged things. They are still functioning very well on the basis of a very simple childish fallacy that it is better to give than to get. And if you want things to go well with you, you think about giving, especially to the church. And those that are only thinking of getting, of course, have all kinds of difficulties: financial and social and everything. So it is possible to be successful on the basis of a false notion of the truth. Because it seems very simple. Everybody is interested in getting. Now, the truth is, if you are seeking to get, you become isolated, you lose all your friends, and you become socially ineffectual. If you want to be generous and to give, everybody will love you. If we were here for the purpose of popularity, then we could do what many rich people do; they donate a lot of money to all kinds of causes and become famous and popular and go to charity balls. And then there are great givers who give millions for charity. But from an existential standpoint this is nothing, absolutely nothing. It is all based on the idea that we are here to confirm ourselves. Self-confirmation is the supreme good of life in the thinking of unenlightened people who cannot recognize that to give or to get, to be right or to be wrong, is all the same. So, isn't it fantastic to consider that many successful projects are based on an ignorant notion of the truth? And they are very knowledgeable about the Bible and their lectures make a lot of sense. They mostly base themselves on history, the history of Christianity that explains the development of ideas. And then they have this one thing, which is that surely Jesus Christ will soon come and save the world. He will come on a white horse. He may be taking equestrian lessons.

Student: Dr. Hora, if one of the things that we say is that "by their fruits ye shall know them," (Matthew 7:20) how do we explain the fact that they do so well from an invalid...

Dr. Hora: Now, the question is: Is doing well financially and socially good fruit? Certainly in the eyes of most people it would appear that this is good fruit...right? Now is it? What do you think?

Student: Sounds pretty good to me. They have a lot of money and are happy and healthy. I don't know how many there are like that, but if it's true that they are happy and healthy and peaceful and having good lives, it doesn't sound too bad.

Dr. Hora: Yes, and good sex.

Student: Okay.

Dr. Hora: Well of course this is nothing. Within the context of the dream of life as a human person, this is nothing because the dream is just a dream. Good and bad, strong and meek, right and wrong, rich and poor, it's all the same. Isn't that strange?

Student: Well, when you say it is all the same, it sure sounds strange to me. If one had a choice between every one of those options—richer, poorer, same; okay, I'll take rich. They are the same, maybe in that you identify them as part of the dream. So by definition they are the same. In terms of living a life they are not the same, right? I mean from the standpoint of the definitions of Metapsychiatry they are the same, but from the standpoint of the world they are opposite.

Dr. Hora: Right.

Student: I am not quite sure what that all means.

Dr. Hora: It means that the dream is still a dream, whether it's a good dream or a bad dream.

Student: Dr. Hora, what is real generosity then? I mean, what is a valid alternative? If generosity is spiritual, then what is the right gift? You were mainly talking about financial giving, right? But if we are interested in living the right way, then generosity seems like a valid quality, a valid value. How do you see that correctly?

Dr. Hora: A lot of giving is disastrous.

Student: Whether it's financial or even friendliness?

Dr. Hora: Yes. But the fact is that giving is not good and getting is not good. Everything within the dream of life as a human person is based on the assumption of self-confirmatory ideation. If we give, we give for ourselves. If we get, we get for ourselves. Therefore giving is not valid and getting is not valid. What is valid? Nobody knows?

Student: Loving.

Dr. Hora: Loving? What is that? You can be loving in a self-confirmatory way.

Student: What is really true? If we think that we have done some wonderfully generous thing but we are still thinking about the fact that we've done the giving, then there are strings attached. It's conditional, and there is always an aftermath that's troublesome. So it's really important to learn the right way.

Dr. Hora: Yes. Isn't this a conundrum?

Student: But then you can't say, "Well, I am not going to give anything."

Dr. Hora: You can say that. It's still the same. You can say a lot of good is being accomplished in the world through philanthropy and through generosity of giving. You know there are big hospitals being built everywhere and marble palaces. If you see that place in California, it's just like a dream, with marble columns and neo-Greek architecture. Everything is just like a Hollywood set. They have concerts there and art and education and everything. Who could think that there is anything invalid about it? It is beautiful, socially desirable, everything is very good. Even our friend here would like it. But that's not reality. And if something is not reality, how can that be any good? A dream is just a dream. As I said to you, a good dream is still a dream. A nightmare is a dream. A good dream is also a dream. What have you got? You have to wake up and you find that this has never been there. Don't we know the story of the shepherd boy, the story of the key flower? You don't remember this?

There was a little shepherd boy who was in the field with his sheep. As he was walking around after the sheep he picked up a little flower and began contemplating this little flower. As he did it, suddenly a big cave opened up on the side of where he was. He never saw this cave before. He was surprised and so he went exploring the cave, and to his amazement he found that the cave was full of treasures—diamonds and gold and silver. All kinds of treasures were in this cave. He got very excited and he started stuffing the precious metals and jewels into his pockets and under his shirt and grabbed as much as he could. In the process he dropped this little flower. Then he heard a voice that said, "ah ah ah, it's all right, it's all right; just don't forget the most important thing." But he wasn't listening, of course, because he was too excited. He filled himself up with these treasures and ran out of the cave. As he got out of the cave, the doors of the cave slammed shut. He looked around and he found that all his treasures turned into dried weeds. He forgot the most important thing, the key flower. What was the key flower? It was the symbol of reality, of divine reality. Very often, when we have a good dream or we make a killing in the stock market or socially become famous, we forget about God. Our good fortune is just setting us up for disaster. This is what happens when we don't know the difference between reality and dreams.

Now you can say, well, if you go to Pasadena, to Ambassador College, it's tangible; you can hug it and hold it. It's real; Ambassador College is real. Oh, no, it's a key flower; it's just a flower that will wilt away. That's not reality. So you see, we have to wake up and we have to reach beyond the dream. You may have heard about this before *Beyond The Dream*.

Student: How can we tell the difference between a good dream and reality? How can we tell when we are participating in reality as differentiated from a good dream?

Dr. Hora: Well, the important point is, of course, to learn to be aware of our self-confirmatory inclinations. Whatever is self-confirmatory isn't real. But beyond that, we have to discover one fact: that giving and getting is invalid. Only spontaneous responding is reality. Because when we respond to manifest needs in the world, it is God who does it. "Of mine own self I can do nothing."(John 5:30) A self-confirmatory form of generosity is nothing; it's a key flower. Responsiveness is the enlightened way of spontaneous, beneficent participation in God's kingdom. Non-personal, non-self-confirmatory benevolence, spontaneously flowing out of an enlightened consciousness, is reality, because it's non-personal, because it's God. Last week we spoke about spontaneity. This is a continuation of that meditation on spontaneity. Once we understand responsiveness, we are neither giving nor getting. We are not right and we are not wrong. We are not winning and we are not losing. We are just transparencies through whom God is manifesting Himself as infinite good. And we discover that it is good to be good. It is very strange. Nobody ever thought of that. People will say it is good politics to be good... right? Nobody will say it is good to be good because God is good. And if we are good, it is God who is good. Only the good that God gives is good. You see? We dispel the dream of yes and no and this and that, all the dualisms that belong in the domain of dreams, because essentially the issue there is self-confirmatory ideation. When Jesus says you have to overcome the world, what does he mean? It means to wake up and realize that God is all there is and we are here to be transparencies for God. So we are not giving anything and we are not getting anything. We are responding. Isn't it simpler? But if we are preoccupied with self-confirmatory thoughts, we don't know how to respond. We talk on the basis of calculative reasoning which sometimes seems reasonable but most of the time is unreasonable.

So, in the final analysis only God is generous. Man is really not capable of generosity. Man is always building himself up as a person. He wants to get credit. He wants to be looked up to. He wants to exercise power. He wants to be famous. He wants to be liked or disliked. It's all the same. Whether we are liked or disliked, it's the same…isn't it? Once we understand self-confirmatory ideation, we can see that all this is part of the dream of life as a person. Ecclesiastes sang about "…vanity of vanities; …all is vanity and vexation of spirit." (Ecclesiates 1:2,14) Self-confirmation confirms itself and all that results is vexation of spirit. Yet when Jesus spoke about reality, his disciples said, "These are hard sayings; who can bear it?" (John 6:60)

Student: What did he say?

Dr. Hora: What did he say? Nothing. He let them walk away. He never tried to convince anybody. We are much more foolish than he was.

Student: Well, does our salvation depend on understanding that?

Dr. Hora: Absolutely. How else will you wake up unless you understand? There would be another way, the Zen way of beating people over the head until they wake up. But we don't have to do that; life does it to us all the time.

So, the founder of the Pasadena Church, the Worldwide Church of God, thought that he could figure it out and that it is very simple. Just give and don't worry about getting. And of course the Bible says something very seductive when it says, "Give, and it shall be given to you; good measure, pressed down...shall men give into your bosom." (Luke 6:38) You are familiar with this quotation, no? "Give, and it shall be given to you; good measure, pressed down, and shaken together, and running over, shall men give into your bosom." (Luke 6:38) What does this mean? This is really a very seductive quotation. Nobody understands it?

Student: Well, clearly if it's seductive, then I don't understand it.

Dr. Hora: Yes, in the Bible there were certain scribes who didn't understand it. They heard it, they wrote it down and it remains in the Bible. It is a mistake when it says that if you are going to give, you are going to get. Therefore give, and people will be generous to you. But you know in the old days they didn't have weights and measures; they had tin cups of various sizes. And what people brought was food and vegetables and corn and whatever. They were giving and getting. If you were giving, people returned to you large measures. If you got a tin cup with, let's say corn, and the corn was shaken together to fill up this container, and then they pressed it down so that more would be heaped up, that's what the Bible described: "Give, and it shall be given to you; good measure, pressed down, and shaken together, and running over, shall men give into your bosom." What is this bosom business? Usually women went to the market and they held the produce. They didn't have plastic shopping bags. There were no shopping bags. They held the goods into their bosom. That's the way it was. Now this becomes a seductive passage because it encourages people to think in terms of giving and getting. And there are various places in the Bible recorded by unenlightened scribes who didn't attend a Metapsychiatric conference. They didn't understand and they thought you have to be generous in order to get a return, because life seems to be that way, involving giving and getting as the dream of life as a person in interpersonal relationships.

Not many people have reached the level of understanding that giving and getting is a dream of life as persons. Now if we are to live our lives in a better dream, because that is what most people want, what's the sense? Where do we get it? You can throw away all of our books and all of our tapes; if you don't understand this, you haven't really learned anything. If you are still thinking in terms of giving and getting you haven't awakened to reality. Our whole economic system is based on giving and getting. But really it is mostly steal and return or something like that. Essentially everything is dualistic on the human plane. But it's not real; it's a dream.

Student: If giving and getting is dualistic, I can understand that. Then is all generosity dualistic? Is generosity and giving the same?

Dr. Hora: All personal generosity is just giving.

Student: But when we give personally, are we being generous in hoping for something in return?

Dr. Hora: Absolutely, in a self-confirmatory way.

Student: So the issue is the enhancement of the self.

Dr. Hora: Of course. You want a plaque somewhere on a building. If you give 25 million dollars, they build you a school or an orphanage. Of course we don't say that it shouldn't be, but we say this is still a dream.

Student: That's giving in expectation of fame.

Dr. Hora: Recognition or perhaps getting into heaven or getting a high position in the church or in the club.

Student: So, it's giving in expectation of getting something personal in return?

Dr. Hora: Absolutely.

Student: But giving as part of one's being, isn't that generosity without any anticipation of anything in return?

Dr. Hora: Yes. We speak about responding to the manifest needs in the world. If it's non-personal, it's prompted by divine love and it can be pennies or millions. It makes no difference.

Student: Or a smile

Dr. Hora: Right. Sure.

Student: There are a lot of examples recently about people who seem to do some heroic things in attempting to fight these floods out in the Midwest. They volunteer to go to places where they've never lived and just go out and work on these dikes and physically do all kinds of things without any personal gain available to them. They are just doing it out of some sense of civic responsibility or whatever. Is that an example of responding or is that people doing it for personal satisfaction? I am not clear if people are doing it to make themselves feel better as differentiated from responding to needs?

Dr. Hora: You will have to bring a list of names.

Student: It can be either. In other words the motivation is the issue, whether the motivation is sincere or honest.

Dr. Hora: Yes.

Student: So what does it mean, "Do unto others as you would have them do unto you?"(Luke 6:31)

Dr. Hora: Well, the Bible is not without mistakes. Actually it was recorded by human beings, unenlightened but well meaning religious people. There are very many passages which deal with the world. "In the world ye shall have tribulation..." (John 16:33) So if we read the Bible as a book about life in the world, it deals with dualism and it deals with self-confirmation. It's filled with all kinds of things. We have to know the difference between reality and dreaming.

Student: That's part of our social order, then. In a way, it kind of keeps us in line on that level.

Dr. Hora: Yes.

Student: But that's not real.

Dr. Hora: We eventually have to overcome the world. That's what Jesus recommended. What happens when we overcome the world? Jesus said "…be of good cheer; I have overcome the world." (John 16:33) Good for him. Now, if we were to see him before he overcame the world and after he overcame the world, what would we have seen? Before he overcame the world, he was just a wandering philosopher, a mendicant, walking around, talking and preaching like a philosopher. What happened to him after he overcame the world?

Student: He ascended.

Dr. Hora: Right. He ceased to be a person. He became a presence, and he still is. Right now his presence is here, whispering words in my ears, which are surprising me too that I can say that. I didn't read this anywhere. I didn't prepare for this. It is coming and it is coming and it is coming and there is no end to it. Isn't that interesting? I never heard such a lecture. I am amazed myself. One day I will disappear and then you will be surprised. I am joking. I am not taking it seriously. Don't be afraid. There was one girl in this group who wanted to hold onto my leg. She was afraid that I would disappear.

There was a line in the Bible that describes when Jesus spoke to some assembly. He finished and he was waiting for questions from the audience and he said that no one dares to ask him any questions anymore. Do you dare ask me?

Student: What do you mean?

Dr. Hora: No one dared to ask him any more questions. They were just wiped out.

Student: Doesn't everybody eventually disappear?

Dr. Hora: Sure. There are big cemeteries everywhere and there are also crematoria. Then there are great disasters where millions of people disappear, from atomic bombs or holocausts. Now, if this would be reality, it would be unbearable. Imagine that six million people disappeared. How can the world remain intact if these were real disappearances—of something that was real before and now it isn't? It would be terrible. Can we say that the Holocaust was not terrible? Certainly it was terrible to all of us who are still in the condition of mental deficiency that we see the world as consisting of three-dimensional objects in space. Somebody asked the Zen master, "What do you say about the Holocaust?" "Six million Jews were murdered," he said. I didn't say it. Nothing happened. You see enlightened life is not experiential. The dream doesn't apply to reality. So no matter what catastrophic experiences we experience, in reality nothing is happening there.

Perhaps some of you saw a Star Trek movie about a year ago or so. Well, Borg came to a community, a very strange community of very placid, peaceful people who were walking around. They looked like vagrants, being rather shabbily dressed, but very peaceful. Weyoun and Klingons came there and they were very hostile and threw bombs on these people, and came and said, "We wiped out the whole community." The leaders of this community sat there around the table and were completely unfazed by this message that there was a mass catastrophe inflicted upon their whole community. And then someone asked them, "Aren't you concerned?" They looked very quiet and they could not understand what he meant. Finally one of the leaders of this community said to him, "Nothing happened; nobody got killed." These were people who were beyond the dream and they were unfazed by the appearances of mass destruction. And their invaders couldn't believe it, and they said, "Well, we are going to kill you too." And they proceeded to attack these few peaceful people. What happened next is that the guns and the weapons that they were going to use on them suddenly became unbearably hot, and they had to drop everything. They couldn't explain what happened. This was a community of people who only used their understanding to take on an appearance of a community of human beings. But actually they had already gone beyond the three-dimensional life form, and they understood that they are not in the dream of personhood. But they had transcended and nothing could touch them. As the Bible says, "No weapon that is formed against thee shall prosper..."(Isaiah 54:17) It was beautifully presented in this Star Trek show. The assumption was that there are communities of people who are not visible to persons, who live among us and who cannot be destroyed because they are in a stage of enlightenment where they know that they are spiritual beings—non-dimensional presences and expressions of God. That was a terrific show. Have you seen it?

Student: Yes.

6

Seriousness

When we turn our attention to the issue of immunity from the effects of gossip, voodoo, witchcraft, influencing and the claims of personal mind power, we are really seeking liberation from mental enslavement. Mental enslavement can be overt, as in mental despotism; or covert, as in mis-education and deceit; or subliminal, as when being exposed to hidden messages suggested through channels reaching us below the level of conscious awareness. Furthermore, mental enslavement can occur through telepathic influences as in cursing and various forms of thought transferences like voodoo, for example. Mental enslavement deprives one of the faculty of responding intelligently and appropriately to issues. For instance, if we are mentally enslaved, we may not be able to respond appropriately to the above enumerated influences, either because our awareness has been impaired by subtle prohibitions against being intelligent, or by outright commands to be stupid. In such cases the victim does not know that he is a victim. Many lives have been ruined through these kinds of nefarious influences. The second possibility is that an individual may be aware of the crippling influences on him, but finds his rage so overwhelming that he doesn't dare to protest. Such individuals may seek refuge in some compulsive activities or physical illnesses. The third alternative is that the victim may develop a paranoid sense of persecutory fear which in turn incapacitates him socially. To all mentally enslaved people, and there are more of them than meets the eye, Metapsychiatry offers a way to freedom by teaching them how to acquire immunity. One of the most insidious forms of mental enslavement is the mesmerism of seriousness. It is insidious because it claims respectability. If we unmask seriousness, we find that it is a form of intimidation. Once we realize that seriousness is a pretense, and we repudiate it, we may discover joy. Joy is a basic quality of the Living Soul. We must constantly be on guard against being seduced into taking seriousness seriously. Seriousness is the enemy of joy. God has created us to be joyous and loving. The alternative to seriousness is not frivolity or silliness. Frivolity and silliness are the flip side of seriousness. Seriousness is self-confirmatory and frivolousness is also self-confirmatory. Joy, however, is God-confirmatory.

People often say that important issues deserve to be treated seriously. Important issues deserve our careful attention, alertness and intelligence. If we are sufficiently enlightened we refuse to be mesmerized by the claims of seriousness and constantly turn our attention towards joy and love we will be beneficial presences in the world and a blessing to others around us. By understanding how to gain immunity from this widespread mental poison we become liberated from its effects, and not only are we protected, but we are also a protection to others.

Seriousness is seductive and contagious. It is a self-confirmatory mode of being. Everything self-confirmatory is contagious, and everything contagious is self-confirmatory. Depressions are forms of seriousness carried to pathological degrees. When seriousness becomes too painful, people often resort to alcohol or drugs. This may lead to short term relief, and long-term serious alcoholism or drug addiction. Tyrannical ideologies, religions, philosophies, and bureaucratic systems of administration tend to use intimidating methods of communication and insist on being taken seriously. When we are faced with important issues and we take them seriously we are really taking ourselves seriously. Important issues must always be approached from the perspective of God and that means with joy, love and intelligence. The Buddha is never serious, but always serene and gently smiling. Gratitude is the door to joy. Seriousness is a killjoy. In order to know what light is, we must be acquainted with darkness; in order to know what joy is we must understand the experience and intent of seriousness. We call this process "cognitive dialectics." Among the many human frailties there is one rather troublesome character trait, namely, self-righteousness. Such individuals insist on being right, no matter how wrong they may be. They also tend to be very serious. There are two kinds of self-righteousness: one wants to be right, and the other wants you to be wrong.

A recent best-seller was entitled: "Winning through Intimidation." Intimidation is so widespread that people are largely unaware of its harmful effects. Its poison manifests itself in fear and psychosomatic disorders. Recently, I met a young lady who was hired by a law firm as a junior employee. The pressures and demands of the mental climate in that office were so devastatingly serious that within a short time, this perfectly healthy young woman came down with what the doctors called "ulcerative colitis." She was then hospitalized and had to face the heavy and serious mental climate of the hospital where she was told that unless she consented to an operation, she would most likely die, because she was "seriously ill." There followed several crippling operations which did not alleviate the problem. Finally, she was advised to seek psychiatric help. Following this advice, her wealthy father found a prominent psychoanalyst who was known for treating serious cases. She entered into psychoanalysis -- by this time she was so fed up with everything serious, that she developed a serious aversion to her psychoanalyst and left him. At this desperate point, she met a childhood friend who happened to be a student of Metapsychiatry. That's when she had her first good laugh! The sun was rising in her life.

The above is not an indictment of the medical profession, but an illustration of the mental poison generated by individuals who take themselves seriously, and insist on being taken seriously. We acquire immunity from the mesmerism of interaction thinking by waking up from the dream of seriousness to the joy and reality of Divine Love. Jesus said, "In the world ye shall have tribulation, but be of good cheer, I have overcome the world." (John 17:33) Furthermore, he said, "Behold, I give unto you power to tread on serpents and on scorpions and over all the power of the enemy, and nothing shall by any means hurt you." (Luke 10: 19) What is this world which Jesus overcame? And what is this power that Jesus can give us? In Metapsychiatry we have come to understand that the world that Jesus spoke of is essentially a dream of interaction thinking. The Third Principle of Metapsychiatry is: "There is no interaction anywhere, there is only omniaction everywhere." Interaction is thought. It is thinking about what others are thinking about what we are thinking. The phenomenal world is thought in visible form. The human body is made up of interaction thoughts. If we listen to what the body is saying we find that it is always speaking about interaction. Jesus teaches us immunity from the poison of serpentine thoughts and biting attacks in malicious relationships (that is the "serpent" and the "scorpion."). In the above mentioned case we can surmise that the body of this woman was saying: "I hate the guts of these employers of mine who are oppressing me and tyrannizing me." That is the Metapsychiatric diagnosis of her particular ulcerative colitis. When we are healthy, the body tends to be silent. We lose sight of the body. If we have a healthy stomach, we don't know that we have a stomach. The Bible says: "It is better to be absent from the body and present with the Lord." (II Corinthians 6, 8) We say it is better to be aware of omniaction than to entertain thoughts of interaction. When Buddha was asked in what way was he different from other people, he replied, "I am awake." Which means that he "overcame the world" of seriousness by progressing beyond the dream of interaction thinking. Jesus said, "Behold, I send you forth as sheep in the midst of wolves; be ye therefore wise as serpents, and harmless as doves." (Matthew 10: 16) When we understand the true nature of seriousness we become immune to it, and at the same time preserve our joy. A beneficial presence in the world is not naïve; he is acquainted with evil, but remains innocent and immune just as Daniel was in the lions' den.

Question: Dr. Hora, how is it that some problems manifest themselves as physical illness and others manifest as mental illness?

Dr. Hora: That is a very interesting question. You will find very little explanation anywhere in the literature, but in Metapsychiatry we have very simple explanations: Where a man's treasure lies, there shall his problems be also. If someone treasures his own mind (which doesn't exist) then his anger will get channeled into his illusory mind, and then we have phenemona of mental disturbances. If someone cherishes his feelings and·emotions, then his anger will be channeled into his affective system and we will find emotional disturbances. If someone is a sensualist or cherishes his physical sensations, then the tendency will be to channel these aggressive and angry thoughts into the physical body and then we have what is called psychosomatlc illnesses. The Bible says: "Thou shalt have no other Gods before me." (Exodus 20:3) The First Principle of Metapsychiatry says: "Thou shalt have no other interests before the good of God which is spiritual blessedness." To be safe, to be healthy, we must cherish spiritual mindedness. "To be carnally minded is death, but to be spiritually minded is life and peace." (Romans 8:6) These are great wisdoms to be appreciated, but not, to be taken seriously!

Comment: Regarding your comment that whoever takes anything seriously is really taking himself seriously—it seems then that seriousness is a function of personal sense or the ego, and therefore where there is no personal sense there is no seriousness. Perhaps the experience of laughter—the release that we all find in it—is that at that moment we transcend ego sense to some degree.

Dr. Hora: Yes. Have you noticed how much we were laughing? And we always do, which is a sign that in these meetings we are rising above and beyond the material, interactional view of life.

7

Selflessness

Student: Dr. Hora, I have a question about being selfless, not being selfish. If you're selfish, is that the same as self-confirmation?

Dr. Hora: But selflessness is not the alternative to selfishness. The alternative to selfishness is unselfishness. There is a tremendous difference, because if you are selfish, you are self-confirmatory, right? If you are unselfish, you are also self-confirmatory. You say, "I am unselfish." Yes? Selflessness is a whole 'nother smoke.

Student: What is selflessness?

Dr. Hora: Could you explain it?

Student: I'd like to understand it.

Dr. Hora: Now, how did we define perfect love?

Student: Nonpersonal, nonconditional benevolence.

Dr. Hora: All right. So selflessness is a conscious awareness of not being a person, not being a self.

Student: Conscious awareness of not being a person.

Dr. Hora: What are we when we are selfless?

Student: Nondimensional?

Dr. Hora: Yes, yes, but more than that.

Student: Are we awarenesses?

Dr. Hora: Awarenesses, yes. Awarenesses of not being a self. But we are just saying what we are not.

Student: We are conscious.

Dr. Hora: We have to be something, right? A selfish person is a self-confirmatory individual, is always thinking about himself, "what am I accomplishing; how am I doing?" Mayor Ed Koch used to ask, "How'm I doing?" All right, so, the opposite of selfishness is unselfishness. There are very good, religious people, good Christians, who are very unselfish, which means they are do-gooders. Yes? They do unto others. Being here for others. The selfish individual is here for himself, which is normal—nothing unusual about that. The religious individual, sincere as he may be, is unselfish, which means he is here for others, right? But selflessness is an entirely different quality of being and comprehension.

Student: Dr. Hora, if we are considering ourselves as not considering ourselves, is that the same as selflessness or is that still not being selfish? Is that still in the duality? I mean, if you are thinking about yourself at all, is that still unselfish?

Dr. Hora: How does that selfless individual think of himself?

Does that stump you? No, not if you have read any of these books lately. (laughter) You may need refresher courses.

Student: You can ask yourself, "Who am I?"

Dr. Hora: Exactly. "Who am I, what am I, where am I," right? And "What is my purpose in life? What is my identity? What is my substance? Where am I located, and What am I doing here?" (laughter) That's funny, isn't it? "Who's on first, and who's on second?" (laughter) So how does a genuinely self-less individual see himself and see life in general? Now, the enlightened individual knows exactly what it means to be selfless.

Once I was walking around the house and I saw some garbage on the ground and I passed it by, chose not to see it. Then I stopped and I said, "There is this garbage. If I am not going to pick it up, who *will* pick it up?" I couldn't pick it up because that would be self-confirmatory, I couldn't refuse to pick it up because that would also be self-confirmatory. So that's a quandary, right? I could neither pick it up nor not pick it up. In either case, I would be confirming myself. First I would say, "I'm a slob," and then I would say, "I am a good boy." (laughter) "I hope somebody sees it that I am picking up this garbage." Isn't that how we reason? No. How does a selfless individual pick up the garbage without confirming himself?

Student: By being issue-oriented.

Dr. Hora: What does that mean?

Student: Well, the issue is that the garbage on the ground doesn't belong there, I guess.

Dr. Hora: Who says it doesn't belong there?

Student: Well, either it goes against aesthetic sensibilities or, if it's a banana peel, someone might trip over it, or whatever. But it's an issue.

Dr. Hora: If this man were to slip on the banana peel, who would be to blame? Another self? Isn't this an interesting question?

Student: By replacing all these ideas with the value, the spiritual value in our home: We'd like to live in harmony.

Dr. Hora: Who is this who likes and does not like? (laughter)

Student: Well, it's intelligence.

Dr. Hora: This conversation reminds me of the Talmudic scholars, the disputations of the theologians: How many angels can you put on the tip of a needle? Well, this is a very instructive example. I hope you appreciate it. (laughter) Okay, so when an enlightened individual walks in his yard and sees this garbage on the ground, who is going to pick it up?

Student: But, he's impelled.

Dr. Hora: Who?

Student: The individual is impelled. He's not really picking it up; there is something beyond him that is talking to him and saying something beautiful to him so that...

Dr. Hora: This is beautiful garbage. (laughter)

Student: Intelligence impels him to pick it up and he, as an individual, isn't involved in the act. It is just a response to this voice of goodness that he is hearing.

Dr. Hora: Yes, you are close to explaining it. Who is picking up the garbage in your place? (addressing a student) What do you think? Who is picking up the garbage at *your* place?

Student: (pointing) She is; unless she impels me to do it. (laughter)

Dr. Hora: Self-confirmatory interaction, that's double trouble. (laughter)

Student: Omniaction is doing it.

Dr. Hora: Omniaction, who is he?

Student: The thoughts that are coming from God through us.

Dr. Hora: In other words, a spiritual value is doing it. The love of order and harmony is doing it. Have you ever seen the love of order walking around the house lately? The secret of this kind of housecleaning is that there is nobody to show off, and nobody gets tired. It's totally effortless, efficient, and effective.

When an individual understands that he is a transparency for God and he is imbued with spiritual values, and it is the spirit that moves him to be in this world as a beneficial presence, not as a person, a garbage collector, he is a presence. A presence is divinely governed and everything he thinks and everything he does and what he responds to is under the impact of the divine value system. So the enlightened man removes whatever is not harmonious and beautiful and good. And there is neither self-confirmation nor self-denial. It just takes place. So there is someone there who is nobody, and this nobody is a wonderful presence, and his home and surroundings are always in perfect order, because order is a spiritual value. That's the life; that's the modus operandi of an enlightened individual. Is this clear to everybody? Yes?

Student: There is a qualitative difference from what I had said earlier about liking harmony. The whole point is: If the individual loves harmony, then that allows the intelligence to come through the individual, as opposed to it's being the person who likes the harmony, because we can appreciate harmony in a personal way or a spiritual way.

Dr. Hora: If you are not a person, you cannot appreciate anything in a personal way, but it fills you with a sense of the glory of the presence of divine Love-Intelligence, which governs everyone, ideally. We are divinely governed. Immortal Mind governs all, and this must be understood—that we are instruments of God. We are not persons, because whatever a person does is always good and bad at the same time. Did you know that? Good and bad. That's why St. Paul said, "The good which I would, I do not, and the evil which I would not, that I do."(Romans 7:19) It's a personal existence, it's totally self-contradictory. We can never do anything just right. Nothing in the human approach to life is right. It's always good and bad. So freedom and peace and wisdom are unavailable as long as we think that we are persons. Unselfishness is a religious attitude; most religions advocate being unselfish. It doesn't work.

Student: It's the idea of being here for others?

Dr. Hora: Yes, right. So, when we speak of perfect love and perfect being, we say it is nonpersonal, nonconditional benevolence.

Student: How does this apply to this situation? I take piano lessons now, and am practicing this little piece, and I pretty much have the notes, but for the life of me, as I often tell the teacher, I don't hear any music. So then the teacher takes a chance; she is very accomplished, and she just plays it. She makes mistakes, but it sounds like music. I don't know how to read music, in the sense that all I see is a bunch of notes and she says I have to understand what the notes mean. I have no idea what notes mean. This must have something to do with harmony. Seems to me you can't do it on a human level. So, how would what you are talking about apply to this situation?

Dr. Hora: Can't your teacher help you, explain to you…?

Student: Well, she gives me all these examples. She plays along with me. She'll play at one end of the piano, and I will play at the other. Sometimes she sings, which helps, and then, as I'm playing she calls to me, "Now do this, stronger" —all these techniques. Yesterday I went through this with her for about half an hour. She told me, "Move over; let me show you how to play it." I walked out of there and I said, "I don't know how to play this; it's a different piece altogether." There must be something over and above memorizing notes and these techniques, in order for somebody to see these notes and play music. Whereas here and there I hear a couple of measures that might sound like something, it all comes back to just the random playing of notes, and there is no enjoyment in it.

Dr. Hora: Can anyone offer some clarification?

Student: Well, the more spiritually minded you become, and the more you love what we are learning here, the more beautiful your music becomes; it just seems to go hand in hand. And it isn't really something you can *do*; you just find that suddenly your music is beautiful and it comes from your soul. It doesn't come from your fingers, it comes from some beauty that is deep inside that wants to express itself, and it's just the same as the other things you described. It suddenly emerges. It sort of "obtains" on the piano, like things obtain in consciousness—you find it there.

Dr. Hora: Does your teacher explain these things to you?

Student: Well, I am very fortunate that this teacher that I have now doesn't know about Metapsychiatry, but practices it. She explains certain things. But I learned how to play beautiful music from sitting next to this woman and listening to what she said and hearing her play the piano, and it just suddenly—I know exactly what he is talking about, I used to play notes, and I don't anymore.

Dr. Hora: Many people complain about this difficulty, especially with the piano.

Student: I used to say exactly what [the other student] is saying, "How do you get this; how can it sound; what is happening?" No, my teacher never verbalized that. But you are sort of drawn to this beauty. And then, it was a fabulous surprise, every once in awhile, little by little I began hearing beautiful music.

Dr. Hora: It is very similar with the ability to discern meanings. Many students of Metapsychiatry complain, "I read all the books, I come to see you, and I know all the answers, and yet when I am faced with a problem, the meaning doesn't seem to come." Right? How do we tune in on a meaning?

Student: Dr. Hora, you said a few months ago, there is a passage, "I shall now turn aside to see what it is." And that seems to help.

Dr. Hora: Yes, that is an interesting point. Moses said that from Mt. Sinai, I think. He saw the burning bush, and he couldn't figure it out, how this bush could burn and not get consumed, right? Because according to physical laws, whatever is burning has to get consumed by the fire. But here was something that was burning but didn't get consumed. So he couldn't figure it out, how such a thing was possible. But then he got an idea. "I will now turn aside and see this great sight . . ." (Exodus 3:3) What did he mean?

Dr Hora (turning to another student): Do you play the piano? Are you a musician?

Student: This conversation has brought something to my attention, an experience that I had when I got married. I moved my piano into the home where my husband and I lived. I used to play all the time, and now I almost never play.

Dr. Hora: How do you explain that?

Student: I think it's just a case of self-consciousness. I think I am expected—

Dr. Hora: Fear of criticism, is that it?

Student: Yes.

Dr. Hora: Now that can stop anybody, the fear of criticism. In the old days they used to demand that the student practice scales from morning 'til night, always the scales, until he got so fed up with the scales that he started to find beauty in the scales. You were glad to discover something in playing the scales. You can find beauty in the scales. For instance, you can enjoy the difference between a C sharp scale and a C minor scale. You can hear a tremendous difference. And little by little, you begin to discover music. Can you tell the difference between C sharp and C minor when you hear it?

Student: I can tell minor from major.

Dr. Hora: Yes, okay. Once you begin to appreciate it, you can begin to hear something. Maybe that helps; I don't know, I never had these lessons. I never took any piano lessons, I just played. I never took any Metapsychiatry lessons. (laughter)

Student: We're in different categories.

Student: What is this phenomenon about fear of criticism?

Dr. Hora: Fear of criticism? That is concern with self. It's self-concern. It's a desire to be praised or to be admired, or to be appreciated, even. All this is nonsense. It is not necessary, and we can rise above it and discover the art of garbage collection. Turn it into a real art.

He has to listen and listen and he suddenly may discover such a thing as music. Before that, he just hears noises. And when you can hear music, you can hear the thoughts the composer had when he was inspired to write down this music. Meaning is the same way. You cannot figure out the meaning of anything. When you study you can reach a point where meanings are just constantly reaching your consciousness and everything is very clear. There is no effort involved. In music you think you are hearing music with your ears. In seeking to understand meanings you think that your brain will figure it out. No, when you hear music it's not with the ears; it's with the soul. And when you discern meaning, again, it's the soul, the divine consciousness. It is awakened in us, just as the Bible says, "Awake thou that sleepest, arise from the dead and Christ shall give thee light." (Ephesians 5:14) It's like the light goes on in your consciousness when you can really hear a piece of music which speaks to you. Sometimes you get goose bumps, and this happens, and the more we are interested in hearing music and in discerning meanings, the more it grows. So something opens up within us and we are available to it. We are conscious of it, and it is a wonderful awakening. The best way to describe it is as an inner awakening.

Now in meditation, it is awareness that awakens within us—the awareness of the Truth of Being. Now, today we hit upon the issue of becoming aware of the nonpersonal modes of functioning by collecting garbage without collecting it but through its being removed, but not by the person. Most garbage is removed by persons. Therefore, the next day it's back again. But enlightened garbage collection is a whole different process.

Student: Remember when I had so much garbage to be collected that the garbage men wouldn't even take it?

Dr. Hora: I remember you had to hire a carting company to empty your closets. Yes, I remember it well. That was the possessive period. (laughter)

Student: Dr. Hora, you were saying before that people can read a lot of spiritual material and not quite get the spirit of it. So what is it if you don't feel you are progressing in the spirit of Metapsychiatry?

Dr. Hora: Now, that is the great blessing of our studies in Metapsychiatry. Because once you get the whiff of meanings, it will awaken in you an appreciation of music, of art and of harmonious coexistence with the world. If you have not yet awakened to meanings, these words are just words, like a piano is just a typewriter. It's a big typewriter, you don't hear the music. Similarly, if we are not able to discern meanings, we have not yet awakened to the spirit. So "it is the spirit that quickeneth; the flesh profiteth nothing." (John 6:63) That is what Jesus meant when he said that. This is the process of inner awakening, and the secret code that opens this door is interest. See, you are very interested in playing the piano, so the next time you are in a bar where there is a piano and there is a little drinking going on, you could sit down and show the folks that you can play, right? (laughter)

Student: One time years ago I was staying at a place that had a bar that had a piano. I would sit down there in the morning and practice a little bit. Nobody but the bartender was there at that hour, and he had the jukebox on. Well, he thought, a guy is playing the piano, so he turned the jukebox off; then ten minutes later, he turned the jukebox on again. (laughter)

Dr. Hora: Motivation is very important, too, but this is beyond motivation. It's a matter of really developing the capacity to hear. To be interested in hearing music we have to be interested in understanding the meaning of our problems. Every day there is an opportunity to discern meanings, because every day we have problems, right? And if we are able to discern the meanings, this is a great blessing. We have a sense of assurance. There's nothing to be afraid of; all you have to know is what the heck is going on in the secret recesses of the mind.

Student: This is really still a problem. I said to Dr. Hora in a private session today that when I am here, I have no fear of anything, and I am so peaceful and I am so aware that there is no fear, and nobody is suggesting to me anything bad—quite the contrary. Now, sometimes I come here and I have just gotten myself into a very frightened or agitated state. I know the first principle; I know that you have to pray ceaselessly and that the first principle is so important. I don't understand what happens to me. I get scared.

Dr. Hora: When you leave here, you are in the world. And in this world you shall have tribulations. When you are here, perhaps you think every problem has a meaning and it is not necessary to be afraid. Because once we know the meaning of our problems, we have no fear. We just see the error of thoughts, and it can be replaced with the truth, and that gives us a sense of assurance. And then we have peace, assurance, gratitude, and love. So when you know that this is a possibility, this is a very comforting thought.

Student: Fear is indicative of the fact that we have shifted toward self-concern as opposed to the focus on spiritual values.

Dr. Hora: Yes, that certainly is true.

Student: I wonder how this can happen—I go from being aware of meanings and that every problem has a meaning to times when I can become hypnotized to the point that I think a problem is a problem with no meaning. There can be a headache, and I can say, "Oh, I have a headache," and it doesn't occur to me immediately to regard it as the physical manifestation of a thought. And then I have to go through the whole thing, from square one, of saying, "Wait a minute, this isn't just a headache; there is a mental counterpart." You've got to ask, "What is the meaning?" I find it so amazing that I can completely forget all that and become hypnotized by the symptoms. So is that just not being willing to face that there is a meaning, that there is ignorance?

Dr. Hora: Yes, right. We are naturally ignorant, because we think that we are natural people and just human. And it is natural for a human being to live in fear. But the Bible says, "God has not given us a spirit of fear but of power and of love and of sound mind." (2 Timothy 1:7) When we are fearful, we have no sound mind. We are disturbed. We are not aware of the Truth of Being. So we say we have to practice meditation—sincere contemplation of the truth of being—all the time, because therein lie all the answers. That way we can overcome the world. How do we overcome the world? What does it mean to overcome the world? Hitler tried it. He had to exterminate millions of people to overcome the world and he designed it according to his own fantasies; and there are many would-be Hitlers in the world. And throughout history there always were—some tried to overcome the world. And Jesus said, "Yes it is possible to overcome the world, but not that way."

How do we overcome the world? Really, how do we overcome the world?

Student: By losing interest in it?

Dr. Hora: By losing interest in the world. What would happen if we lost interest in the world?

Student: We'd suffer from apathy—lack of energy and enthusiasm.

Dr. Hora: You mean we would become apathetic, right? Then we would probably be missing the world. That's what depression really is. Many people suffer from depression because they cannot cope with the world and something is missing. Some essential element in life. You see, there is a difference between losing interest in the world and overcoming the world.

Student: Dr. Hora, you always said the world is really interaction thinking and self-confirmatory ideation. So, if we know that definition, that's what heals the pain.

Dr. Hora: Exactly. It is very important to understand that the world consists of two elements. It's very simple: yes and no. And these two elements are self-confirmatory ideation and interaction thinking. When we are able to transcend these human tendencies that make us natural people like everybody else, then we have overcome the world, and what we have left is peace. But who needs it? What the world wants, really, is excitement, right?

Student: When we talk about fear it can be so all-pervasive, a general problem. If we ask, "What is the meaning of fear?" we might say that it is self-concern, a power apart from God. But must we be more specific then that? I think there is acute fear, and then there is an all-pervasive fear, existential fear, an uncomfortableness. So how do you decide...?

Dr. Hora: That is a very good point, because we cannot settle for clichéd answers. You know what a clichéd answer is? Something that we read *about*. Now, if fearfulness is our problem, then we have to meditate and wait until the specificity of that experience reveals itself to us completely. Because every fear has a special meaning. There is a universal meaning to it, but there is something special individually. Very often fear torments us because we want something. And we don't like to face the fact that we want something, because if we want something, we really want it. And who wants to give up what he wants? So it becomes very difficult to be interested in the meaning of our private fear.

Student: Dr. Hora, because if we face it, then we also face the fact of giving it up?

Dr. Hora: Yes, of course. And everybody has something special, some private quirk of what he wants, and to know the meaning of it is to lose interest in what we want.

Student: Wants are pretty universal, I mean, we want to control, we want...

Dr. Hora: Yes. Now the interesting thing about want, which is reminiscent of what we started today's session about, is when somebody is told, "Look here, you are suffering these agonizing fears because you want something." If he is a very good student, he'll say, "Okay, so I won't want it. I will not want what I want. I'll give it up."

Student: Then he'd become *really* fearful.

Dr. Hora: Can you see how tricky this is? You cannot say, "Is this my problem, that I want something? So I won't want it. Am I healed now?" Of course not, right? Who needs Metapshychiatry if everything is so easy? Suppose that what you want is popularity. You want popularity. It fills you with anxiety, you struggle with it, you go to see your psychiatrist and he says, "The trouble with you is that you want popularity." And you say, "Okay, so I will give up wanting popularity." And then you find that nothing happens, you are just as scared as ever. Yes? So what is the solution?

Student: We have to become interested in some healthy value, genuinely interested. And that obliterates the interest in what we want.

Dr. Hora: Right. We cannot give up something. We have to replace it.

Student: There is no such thing as fear without wanting something?

Dr. Hora: Absolutely not. Behind every fear there is a want. Because I want security, I want assurance, I want happiness. I want somebody to drop dead. We have all kinds of wants.

But first we have to be very sincere and willing to face up to this peculiar thing that we want something, and then we have the problem: how to be free of this wanting.

Student: Is apathy not wanting?

Dr. Hora: Apathy is a condition in which you have accepted defeat. You say, "Well I give up, I am burned out. I do not want anything, I just want to collapse and feel sorry for myself." And then you have caught yourself in a trap, because when you feel sorry for yourself you want something. You want to enjoy feeling sorry for yourself. So life is a conundrum. There is nothing to want except to see what really is. What *is*, what is?

Man is the image and likeness of God, a transparency for God's qualities. Isn't it possible for us to want the truth? Wouldn't that solve the problem? So you say, "I don't want popularity, I want the truth." Unfortunately you cannot want the truth. If you want the truth, you are a failed theologian. At best, we can be *interested* in knowing the truth. That's the universal feeling for the occasion, because every time we catch a glimpse of the truth, something gets healed in us. Because it is only the truth that sets us free.

It's very elusive, the truth. You cannot sink your teeth into it, you cannot hold on to it, you cannot grab it, you cannot force yourself to it. But you can become interested in knowing the truth, being aware of the truth, which is God and its perfect universe, infinite love and intelligence. And every time this truth becomes more important to us, and as we become more and more interested in it, there is something getting healed. And it's the healing remedy for every possible problem.

And nobody can give it to us. We cannot say, "Help me to know the truth." You can say it, but it is difficult. It requires absolute interest. We really have to reach the point where we are more interested in knowing the truth of perfect God and perfect man as His creation, be more interested in that than anything else. So Jesus said, "I am the way, the truth, and the life." "I am the door; by me, if any man enter he shall be saved" "and he will find pasture," (John 14:6; 10:9) and that is his salvation.

8

Seeing God vs. Ignorance

Student: Dr. Hora, the other day I went to the supervisor's office to ask about some books I wanted to refer to. I couldn't find the books, so I was about to ask her, "Where are the books?" I couldn't find my voice, so I cleared my throat, but I still couldn't find my voice.

Dr. Hora: It was with the books maybe.

Student: When I finally questioned her, "Where are the books?" it came out in an unclear fashion. So I asked the meaning, and I think I bear some resentment toward this supervisor.

Dr. Hora: Right, right, so?

Student: I can't seem to get past resentment. So maybe this is the question: How does one transcend resentment toward this supervisor?

Dr. Hora: Before you say hello, you tell yourself not to be thinking of anything else. You remind yourself that right now you love her, and you are interested in remaining positively attuned to this individual.

Student: If I were to say something like that, I don't think I would understand it. And since I don't understand it, I fall into a nice guy approach, which, from what I have seen, this woman takes advantage of. "You do it; you're a nice guy." Yeah, I am a cooperative worker, I'll do it. Next, I find that this is what happens.

Dr. Hora: This is psychology. Did you know that you are an amateur psychologist? It doesn't work; psychology doesn't work. But if your reasoning is based on the acknowledgment of God as infinite presence and love-intelligence, of which you are a representative, this throws an entirely different light on the situation. We're not interested in having nice relationships. We are interested in seeing through the eyes of God, even before you say hello. Everything works together for good to them that love being loving for God's sake. It's nothing personal; you don't have to have a personal relationship with the supervisor. You have to be here for God. Life is so much simpler that way, right? Relationships complicate life terribly.

"I couldn't find my voice," you said. What a strange thing to say. Where do you look for it? It was hidden; just like the books were hidden, your voice was hidden in a secret chamber of hostility and judgmentalism. Right?

Student: Dr. Hora, he's talking about the fact that he harbors ill will toward this woman. He doesn't like her; he's resentful. I understand what's required, but I don't understand how it happens. He needs to see this woman differently, needs to say, "I love you." But he doesn't mean it. So even if he says it anyway, but doesn't mean it, it doesn't get him anywhere. As you say, it turns into psychology. It doesn't work. He's angry because he says that now she takes advantage of him. I'm the exact same way with other people, but the solution that I end up with is just as bad as what he's saying, because it's operational. So I do this and it doesn't work. The notion of right seeing seems to be beyond my ability. And anything that I try to substitute doesn't work because it's all operational. When I go to see this person I'm going to say I love him. So I say to myself, "I love him." But I don't love him. I keep saying I love him but how can you love somebody that you don't love? That's the issue.

Dr. Hora: Well, you need a new pair of glasses. We have to learn to look at life and at people and situations through the eyes of God, not through the eyes of personal opinions. You could also say, "Before I say hello, I have to remind myself of how God sees the individual. I have to see this individual through the eyes of God." Immediately things change. We change. They change. They become what they really are, and we become what we really are, and we become divinely governed. Suddenly, all anxiety disappears. All tension disappears. Suddenly we find our voice; it's right there. We found it. We find the books. Now there is good will on both sides, on every side. Then that's a wonderful situation. There is no need for tension and anxiety in personal relationships. This word "relationship" is anathema to God. There are no "relationships." Relationships are on a seesaw. You know the seesaw? One goes up; the other goes down. All it is is mental strife, a battle for power and superiority of all kinds. So you have to learn to see life through the eyes of God. How does God see life? Perfect. He created it. God created a perfect universe, and peopled it with reflections of Himself. And that's what we have to learn.

Student: So it seems like in this context we get stymied in attempting this by being inauthentic. I may not like or resent this individual, but if I hear what's being said correctly is that there is a much healthier way of looking at things. The other way of looking at things, the relationship way, is always troublesome.

Dr. Hora: Right.

Student: And if we genuinely explore this way of looking at things, then we will see that things will work out.

Dr. Hora: Right, sure. Did everybody hear what he said? It's very true.

Student: I'd like to follow up on what he just said. Sometimes if I become aware of a thought that was expressed by the other students, I can recognize the invalidity of it. And I get a little frightened by the invalid thought, because it's so clear that invalid thoughts have meanings and that meanings express themselves in our lives in very negative ways. So, that's one thing that sort of pushes me in a different direction. But it doesn't seem quite right; it's almost like you're searching for God out of fear. So that doesn't seem quite right. And then I think that you need to just turn to God, because that's the way it is. And you can't fight what is.

Dr. Hora: The Bible says: "The fear of the Lord is the beginning of wisdom." (Proverbs 9:10) This was always very puzzling to people. It still is, as if we would have to be afraid of God.

Student: Well, no, I'm not afraid of God. I'm afraid of invalid thoughts.

Dr. Hora: Godlessness. What we have to be afraid of is God-lessness.

Student: But you said that what the student said is very true, that these thoughts are troublesome. Isn't that wrong too, to seek a better way because of being fearful of invalid thoughts?

Dr. Hora: Well, it's not wrong, but it's inevitable. That's what Metapsychiatry teaches, that we have to be aware of the thoughts which are present in consciousness, their quality and direction and source, everything about them. We need to seek to bring our attention into focus with divine reality. That's all there is. But when you said, "the fear," you were referring to the Bible speaking of the fear of the Lord. No, that is a mistake. We don't' have to be afraid of God; we have to be afraid of Godlessness. And when we are involved in personality conflicts, there is no God in our conscious-ness at that point. And then mistakes happen. There is fear, anxiety, and tension; there is confusion. So, we have to be afraid of Godlessness, interaction thinking, self-confirmato-ry thinking. This is a distraction from God, which is called the devil. The function of the devil is to distract us from the awareness of God and his universe of perfect being. So, when the student has an encounter with a supervisor, they are completely involved in thoughts of relationship, which can be negative or positive. God is not in the picture. No-body is aware of God. And losing awareness of God is a mis-take, a grave mistake. So we have to maintain constant con-scious awareness of God through perfect love and sincere contemplation of the truth of being. With a little luck this is possible. "With a little bit of luck . . . Get me to the church on time." (laughter)

People will ask: What has Metapsychiatry to offer that all

of these tremendous volumes of books about psychology, psychoanalysis, psychotherapy, psycho-this and psycho-that, cannot offer? What have they got that other people haven't got? In what way is this teaching different from all the dignified and admired and erudite and highly respected volumes of books and teachings throughout the world? Why bother with Metapsychiatry? You can be on Fifth Avenue, on Park Avenue, in elegant surroundings in some prestigious salons, with people respected throughout the world for their writings. And thousands of people go to see these people. I heard recently about a professor of economics, a lady professor of economics at New York University, with a husband who was also a prestigious academic. They were going to a very elegant place for psychoanalysis for years and years, and they were always getting worse and worse. They cannot live without each other; without each other they were economically sliding down into a pit. And nothing seems to work. It's no surprise, because without God nothing can work, since God runs the universe. And if you ignore God's presence in his own universe where are you? You're in never-never-land. In Metapsychiatry we learn to see through the eyes of God and to maintain a constant conscious awareness of God's presence as a governing intelligence of life. And we are alert not to allow anything else to distract us from the awareness of God, which is the work of the devil. That's what the devil is here for, to distract us. But then, if there were no devil we wouldn't appreciate the glorious spiritual blessedness of the children of God. Before you say hello, you remind yourself that you're not just another person meeting another person, and managing a relationship. You don't manage a relationship. Is you is or is you ain't? That's the question, right?

Student: Now, I could complain that I have difficulty seeing

God in this situation. But, I could also say it another way, that I am more interested in fostering and hanging onto my resentment than in seeing things in a more spiritual way. Would that be more correct?

Dr. Hora: Well, it's a free country. You can hang onto any kind of matter you like, but does God hang onto resentment? God forbid. Remember that you are not what you seem to be. You are not a human person indulging himself in resentful feelings and thoughts. You are a transparency for God. It is the Father that dwelleth in you, He doeth the works. And as far as your resentments are concerned, you ain't never was nothin'. So we don't have to manage our feelings and emotions and opinions and relationships. We don't have to be involved in this human misery. We just need to learn to see who we really are, the truth of being. And that's what is. And everything that really is, was made by God and is God and is perfect. "Be ye therefore perfect, even as your Father in heaven is perfect." (Matthew 5:48) We don't have to make ourselves perfect; we already are perfect. God made us perfect. And in Metapsychiatry we learn to see this.

Student: Dr. Hora, you are using the word "devil." Is there a definition of the devil, or is that a symbol of whatever is not godly? What is the devil?

Dr. Hora: It's a personification of the evil desire to ignore God. He has two horns and a three-pronged pitchfork. And Christmas is coming soon and you will see him all over the place.

Student: It starts at Thanksgiving.

Dr. Hora: Yes.

Student: Dr. Hora, when you said before that we have to see ourselves as perfect, how does one see oneself as perfect non-personally? How would you regard yourself?

Dr. Hora: Well, you are contemplating the Truth of Being. The Truth of Being is not a physical person; it's a divine consciousness. And that consciousness is supremely intelligent and loving and absolutely perfect—never born, never dying, hid with Christ in God. It already is. Don't worry. This is good. It is absolutely perfect. As the Bible puts it, nothing can be put to it nor taken away from it.

Student: What is it that sees it?

Dr. Hora: God is seeing himself. He has a mirror. He is always looking in a mirror and he sees himself. If you have children you very often see yourself in your children, don't you?

Student: I think a mother probably would.

Dr. Hora: The good and the bad and the stupid and the smart and the male and the female. But we are transparencies through whom God is manifesting himself in the world through an infinite variety of individualities. If the ocean is the spirit, then a snowflake is the soul of an individual. What's the difference between the ocean and the snowflake? It's the same substance. The snowflake has the same substance as the ocean. And yet every snowflake is an individual and different from every other snowflake. Isn't that interesting? Are we all flaky? (laughter)

Some people will say...

Student: Nondimensional spiritual consciousness exists regardless of a dimensional being?

Dr. Hora: Yes. What happens to a snowflake if it melts and falls into the ocean?

Student: It becomes part of the ocean.

Dr. Hora: Did you ever think of it what happens to that individual uniqueness which every snowflake is?

Student: It disappears, right?

Dr. Hora: It seems to but it couldn't possibly. Either it is a unique individual or it isn't. And if a soul is immortal, and even if its formal appearance disappears, still it cannot be lost; it must exist. So if somebody dies and he disappears, we say the soul is immortal and it survives but we cannot see it because it's nondimensional. I think in a computer memory interesting things can happen. Information can disappear, right? And there's no way of seeing it and knowing it except if you know how to call it back, right? And that interferes in its perfection. And while it was in the computer it was nothing, right? There was no way anybody could see it.

Student: Have you experienced this?

Dr. Hora: No, I've listened to my friend who talks computerese. That's a new language. It's fascinating.

Student: It's really interesting because it's invisible.

Dr. Hora: Yes, nobody would suspect that it is there, right? Some times you get surprised by what's coming to you.

Student: Dr. Hora, when you said what is it when a snow flake goes into the ocean, first thing that came to mind is bliss.

Dr. Hora: Bliss?

Student: Bliss. But if we already mean to say, if the analogy is that we're really part of God but we're really separate. But then if we were to see that, it would be blissful.

Dr. Hora: Blissful, certainly. Of course the quality of divine life is spiritual bliss. Bliss consciousness. Or as the first principle says, "Thou shalt have no other interests but the good of God which is spiritual blessedness." When we are in a state of spiritual blessedness, everything seems to be all right. There is nothing to complain about or worry about—or fear. Peace, assurance, gratitude, love. This is the supreme good of life. Lasagna notwithstanding.

Student: I'd like to consider the word PAGL, in a situation like a meeting where people are feeling very pressured. In a meeting where, for instance, a report has to get generated and calculated and it has to be done by a certain time, people urgently need this report. There is a lot of politics going on at the meeting and everyone is jockeying to show they know more than other people. It's a very ugly situation. How can one be aware of God in that situation? It's not that difficult when you're by yourself, but in a meeting with these people where all these things are going on, how can one be aware of God?

Dr. Hora: That's a very good question. Any answers? He describes life as it is experienced in the marketplace, right? In the marketplace, that's how we experience life. But experiences are not real life. Experiences are what we perceive; we perceive the thoughts in the sea of mental garbage. So, how can one transcend these experiences and still remain in business?

Student: Not become a priest.

Student: Deal with the issues, rather than with personalities?

Dr. Hora: Oh, absolutely, that's an absolute requirement. The question is could an enlightened individual function in a meeting place in a bank or anywhere else where normal human crazy people communicate; that's the big, big question. And sometimes it's difficult. Perhaps most of the time it is very difficult. But you can always excuse yourself and go to a private place and contemplate the truth of being and come back refreshed with new ideas. (laughter)

Student: Well, last week in our private session, I asked you, "How could contemplating the truth of being help us transcend what you're describing?" And you said that the truth of being is perfect God and perfect man and that if you're contemplating perfect God and you stick with it, then you begin to see that you can't be anything other than that perfection which God is. You just stay with this until you can in some way see that you are in fact that perfection that God is. And you said that would be a helpful way to function, I guess.

Dr. Hora: Yes. Pretty soon the fear leaves you. See, in such situations people are constantly thrashing at each other, competing with each other and intimidating each other. Now, if you can turn your thoughts to the perfection of God and his universe this gives you new strength. The fear leaves you and you are not upset over what people want. All these things can leave you and suddenly you are normal again.

Student: Well I'm hopeful that something you said tonight makes it easier for me because I found it not possible for me to look at somebody at the meeting and see that person as perfect. It seems to me that you have to be God to see that person as perfect. But tonight you said that another approach might be, instead of saying, "I love you," and not being able to mean it, another way of approaching it would be to think of this person the way God sees this person. That I think would be easier for me. In other words, I can understand I think a little bit how God could see this person as perfect even if I can't. So the fact that I can't, I find so frustrating all the time. I find terrible frustration that I cannot see these other people as perfect or myself as perfect. But I think it may be easier then to see these people the way I can understand that God sees them.

Dr. Hora: Right. This reminds me of a guy who was negotiating with a very high powered manufacturer of elevators. And this fellow tried to negotiate a contact with the elevator guy who was very rough and arbitrary and they couldn't agree on some detail. They left all frustrated that the deal was an impossibility. This fellow was complaining that it seemed impossible because this man is so arbitrary and doesn't budge. He never wants to consider any alternative. It was very upsetting for him, right? And then we talked for a while and threw a new light on the situation and brought God into the picture, yes? What else? And next week, this arbitrary, dictatorial fellow initiated a new negotiation phase and he was friendly and cooperative and the thing was resolved because God, the third party, was in the negotiation. If God isn't there, nothing can work. But if you invite God into the negotiating room you will see the difference. Right? He was that guy.

Student: You never forget him either.

Dr. Hora: If you go into negotiation with someone about business or something and if you assume that this process must be adversarial, then you have already built in the factor of failure because adversarial negotiations never can come to a favorable resolution. But if, before you say hello, you remind yourself this is not an adversarial situation then you're not adversaries. We are spiritual beings seeking the truth which makes everything harmonious and blesses one and blesses the other equally. This whole concept of adversarial negotiations and debating is based on the assumption that "homo homeo lupus." What is that? What is that? Nobody knows Latin here?

Student: Something about the wolves?

Dr. Hora: Men are with each other like wolves, like animals. Adversary, hostile, power mad, destructive. That's the whole concept of adversary. Adversarial relationships. Lawyers have invented it.

Student: Dr. Hora, I'd like to ask a little more about the issue of our uniqueness and when the student said that her first response to the image of the snowflake melting into the ocean was bliss. It seems that I tend to get uniqueness and personhood very confused in my mind. For example, is the Buddha nature when there is a total loss of a sense of self? Does holding onto the idea of bliss, as I heard the other student say, come because it really is a relinquishing of selfhood? But uniqueness and selfhood just are inextricably mixed up in my understanding.

Dr. Hora: Yes. Nobody mentioned selfhood in a psychological sense. We're not selves in a psychological way because self is synonymous with personhood and so we're not persons either. But there is a sense, a sense of selfhood in terms of the uniqueness of each individual. So, like a snowflake, every one of us is a creation of God and everyone is different and yet made of the same stuff. It's like in the Bible there is reference to "the leaves of the tree were for the healing of nations." (Revelation 22:2) That's a mysterious kind of statement. Are they recommending that we use the leaves and put it on roofs? People actually used to do that. But this is a naïve idea. How can you heal the nations of the world with leaves from a tree? Right? It must have a secret meaning. All of the apocalypses were loaded with symbolism that is difficult to understand—it takes a great deal of meditation and study to come to some realization. What is meant by this, "the leaves of the tree are for the healing of nations?" So, the metapsychiatric view of this mysterious thing is that we have to contemplate what a leaf is. The knowledge of what the leaf is, the truth of the being of the leaf can illuminate for us the healing of nations. Namely, you have to understand that every leaf, and there might be a million leaves let's say on a sugar maple tree, and every leaf is different from every other leaf. They are all unique and they never fight except when the wind blows. They coexist harmoniously on that tree and they are made of the same stuff as the tree is made of and they identify the tree. They have their own identity and they are unique and at the same time they are all maple leaves. So we can understand this complicated fact of nature, this phenomenon. A tree teaches us to see that there is such a thing as unique individuality. We're not speaking of self but of unique individuality of soul. And the soul is made of the spirit, is the spirit, just like the snowflake is a uniquely individual manifestation which is made of the same substance as the ocean. Now if it disappears in the ocean, the question is, "Where is it?" Like with the computer. Once you commit something to the computer memory, it disappears. There is no way you can see it anymore. But you can record it. And probably that's what happens to snowflakes too. Next winter you have to shovel it. So, if the nations of the world would understand the leaf, the whole world would be healed. The leaves are for the healing of nations. What is needed for the nations is to understand the leaf. That understanding of the leaf will enlighten the whole world and consequently there will be universal PAGL. Right? PAGL consciousness in the world—wouldn't that be nice? To understand the leaf. There was an Indian guru who said that enlightenment happens to you when you can see the Taj Mahal in a blade of grass. Isn't that an interesting saying? You can see the Taj Mahal in a blade of grass.

Student: What does the Taj Mahal represent?

Dr. Hora: Good question. That's what you have to answer. Then you will understand this koan. What does the Taj Mahal represent? Perfection, architectural perfection, love, because love has built it. Beauty, perfect beauty, that's the Taj Mahal. Only the divine mind could have given rise to such an architectural miracle. And a blade of grass is an architectural miracle which grows spontaneously by the grace of God. Now if you understand such things truly, you're enlightened. The leaves of the tree are for the healing of nations. When we speak of healing in Metapsychiatry we are always speaking of the quality of consciousness. When we heal, there is only one disease; it's called ignorance. And when ignorance is healed it is eliminated from consciousness —then you have a healing. What happens when a leaf severs from the tree?

Student: It dies.

Dr. Hora: It dies. What does that mean? It ceases to be a leaf; it becomes trash. Without God everything is trash.

Student: Even when our body dies?

Dr. Hora: Our body is trash. Surely. Ashes to ashes, dust to dust. But the soul is immortal and lives on in the Ocean of Love-Intelligence. There's the sea of mental garbage, right? And the Ocean of Love-Intelligence.

Other books
by
Thomas Hora

Encounters with Wisdom: Book One

This book is the first of a series of short volumes that present Dr. Thomas Hora's Metapsychiatric teachings through dialogues with his students.

Table of Contents: Spiritual Blessedness ~ The Inside and the Outside ~ Death and Mourning ~ The Meaning of Attachment ~ Abundance ~ What Yen Hui Understood ~ Koans and the Rosetta Stone of Metapsychiatry ~ Spontaneity

135 pages $12.00 ISBN 1-931052-03-4

One Mind, A Psychiatrist's Spiritual Teachings

"The meaning of life is to come to know Reality."—Thomas Hora, M.D.

These dialogues between Dr. Hora and his students first teach us the meaning of our mental, emotional and physical problems, and then point to the Reality of God, the one true Mind in which we live and move and have our being.

As we become aware of our true existence in God, our problems begin to dissolve and we realize peace, assurance, gratitude and love.

Those who are familiar with these teachings and those who are new to them will appreciate and benefit from the inspired wisdom in One Mind.

400 pages $25.00 ISBN 1-931052-01-8

Beyond the Dream: Awakening to Reality

Beyond the Dream contains original insights on life, health, healing and wholeness... insights that can help anyone to awaken spiritually - to find light beyond the dream of life as personal selfhood. Dr. Hora drew on the teachings of Jesus as much as he did on conventional psychotherapy to evolve a way of seeing and being in the world that bears good fruit, here and now.

Beyond Nothingness ~ Transubstantiation ~ Willfulness ~ "Fail-Safe" ~ A
Sense of Humor ~ The Curtain of Fear ~ Sex Education ~ Yielding ~ The
Natural, The Supernatural, and the Spiritual ~ Innocence ~ The Bureaucrat
and the Therapist ~ Safety ~ Marriage and Parenting ~ The Divine Context
~ "The Nightmare Pill" ~ Fearlessness ~ The Love of Being Loving ~ The
Healing Environment ~ The Riddle of the Sphinx ~ Approbation ~ The
Question of Affectivity ~ The Physical is Mental ~ The Healing Factor ~
Malicious Hypnotism ~ Semantics ~ The Body ~ Anger ~ Alcoholism ~
Levels of Cognitive Integration ~ Friction ~ The Other Cheek ~ Anxiety ~
The Origin of Man ~ The Line and the Circle ~ Enlightenment ~ Solitary
Man ~ Decision or Commitment? ~ Guilt ~ Evil ~ Compassion ~ Is There
Nothingness? ~ The "IS" ~ How Mature is God? ~ The Living Soul ~ Prayer
of "At-one-ment" ~ Reading List and Index

ISBN: 0-8245-1636-2; $16.95, paperback, 348 pages.

Dialogues in Metapsychiatry

These dialogues between Dr. Hora and
his shed new light on what is real and
what is illusory, and on such issues as our
purpose in life, the good of life, affluence,
ambition, anxiety, humility, freedom,
safety, and joy.

Table of Contents: The Supreme Way ~ The Perfect
Principle ~ The Real ~ The Right Context ~ Think-
ing and Knowing ~ I Am the Light ~ Meditation ~
Affluence ~ Who is in Control? ~ What is Good? ~ Beholding the Good ~
What is Beholding? ~ Beyond Religion ~ Symbolic Structures ~ What is a
Healing? ~ Freedom and Joy ~ Safety ~ Protection ~ Substance ~ Parasitism
~ Self-Pity ~ Pleasure and Joy ~ Frictionlessness ~ The Human Mockery ~
Eternal Damnation ~ What is the Purpose of Man? ~ What is Life? ~ Over-
coming the World ~ Ambition ~ The Gatekeeper ~ Meekness and Humility
~ Is God Slow? ~ Anxiety ~ Believing and Knowing ~ Indestructible Life ~
Self-Confirmatory Ideation ~ Power Struggle ~ What is Hypnotism? ~ Prog-
ress ~ Is it Worth It? ~ Completeness ~ Self-Esteem ~ Interaction or Omniac-
tion? ~ Innocence ~ Yes is Good ~ No Is Also Good ~ On Being Helpful ~
Parameters of Progress ~ Reading List and Index

ISBN: 0-8245-1637-0; $14.95, paperback, 248 pages.

Existential Metapsychiatry

A companion to *Dialogues in Metapsychiatry*, it is dedicated to "the sincere seekers after the truth who are willing to forego intellectual conformity in exchange for freedom and authenticity ... Dr. Hora presents a therapeutic method based upon the free use of creative intelligence and open-minded receptivity to the patient. His therapy leaves behind all preconceived ideas, explanations, and speculations, especially those based upon cause and effect reasoning. Instead he participates with the patient in a search for truth and understanding resulting in healing and harmony with the fundamental order of existence." (Excerpt from book cover)

ISBN: 0-913105-007; $20.00, 234 pages.

\

In Quest of Wholeness

Table of Contents: Cognition and Health ~ Illness and Health - What Are They? ~ The Transpersonal Perspective ~ Beyond Self ~ Responsibility ~ Wholeness ~ Prayer ~ Identity ~ The Epistemology of Love ~ Commentary on a Lecture at a Scientific Meeting ~ Religious Values in Illness and Health ~ Transcendence and Healing ~ Existential Psychotherapy, Basic Principles ~ Bibliography and Index

$15.00, 141 pages.

Encounters with Wisdom: Book Two

More dialogues with Dr. Thomas Hora and his students.

Table of Contents: Radical Therapy ~ Is You Is or Is You Ain't ~ Freedom and Corruptibility ~ Wanting to Be Right ~ The Wisdom to Know the Difference ~ Reaction vs. Response ~ The Greatest Protection ~ Reverence for Life

138 pages $12.00 ISBN 1-978-1-93105-204-7

To order or for more information

Please call (860) 434-2999
FAX (860) 434-1512
or e-mail PAGLBooks@aol.com